D0265505

David Hare

David Hare was born in Sussex in 1947. His first play, *Slag*, was produced in 1970. A year later he first worked at the National Theatre, beginning one of the longest relationships of any playwright with a contemporary theatre. Since 1978, the National has produced eleven of his plays. Four of his best-known plays, *Plenty, The Secret Rapture, Racing Demon* and *Skylight,* have also been presented on Broadway. The first of his six feature films, *Wetherby,* which he also directed, won the Golden Bear at Berlin in 1985.

by the same author

Plays

PLAYS ONE
(Slag, Teeth 'n' Smiles, Knuckle, Licking Hitler, Plenty)
PLAYS TWO
(Fanshen, A Map of the World, Saigon: Year of the Cat,
The Bay at Nice, The Secret Rapture)
AMY'S VIEW
BRASSNECK (with Howard Brenton)
THE GREAT EXHIBITION
PRAVDA (with Howard Brenton)
RACING DEMON
THE ABSENCE OF WAR
SKYLIGHT

Screenplays for Television

LICKING HITLER
DREAMS OF LEAVING
HEADING HOME

Screenplays

WETHERBY
PARIS BY NIGHT
STRAPLESS
PLENTY
THE SECRET RAPTURE

Opera Libretto

THE KNIFE

Prose

WRITING LEFT-HANDED
ASKING AROUND:
background to the David Hare trilogy

DAVID HARE

MURMURING JUDGES

faber and faber
LONDON · BOSTON

First published in 1991
by Faber and Faber Limited
3 Queen Square London WC1N 3AU
Reprinted with corrections, 1993

Photoset by Parker Typesetting Service, Leicester
Printed and bound in Great Britain by
Mackays of Chatham PLC, Chatham, Kent

A CIP record for this book
is available from the British Library

ISBN 0-571-17219-9

For Richard

Murmuring Judges was first performed at the Olivier Theatre, London, on 10 October 1991. The cast was as follows:

Constabulary

PC SANDRA BINGHAM	Lesley Sharp
PS LESTER SPEED	Paul Moriarty
PC DAVE LAWRENCE	Keith Bartlett
PC TOBY METCALFE	Simon Coates
PC ESTHER BALLY	Sally Rogers
DC BARRY HOPPER	Keith Allen
DC ABDUL 'JIMMY' KHAN	Paul Bhattacharjee

Bench and Bar

JUDGE	Jeffrey Segal
MR JUSTICE CUDDEFORD	Michael Bryant
SIR PETER EDGECOMBE QC	Richard Pasco
IRINA PLATT	Alphonsia Emmanuel
WOODY PEARSON	Tim McMullan
TOASTMASTER	Doyne Byrd

Prison Service

PO RAYMOND BECKETT	Joseph O'Conor

Government

RT HON. CHARLES KENDRICK MP	Peter Wight

Clients

GERARD MCKINNON	Robert Patterson
KEITH MACHIN	Paul Wyett
WOMAN UNDER ARREST	Judith Coke
DAUGHTER	Judy Damas
BANGLADESHI MAN	Royce Hounsell
BANGLADESHI WOMAN	Sandra James-Young

JASON SMITH	Tyrone Huggins
'NELSON'	Walter Hall
FIRST PRISONER	Andrew Woodall
SECOND PRISONER	John Adewole

Police, barristers, court officers, prisoners, defendants, prison officers, etc.

Director	Richard Eyre
Designer	Bob Crowley
Lighting	Mark Henderson
Music	Richard Hartley

This production was revived as part of the David Hare trilogy at the Royal National Theatre, Olivier Theatre, 2 October 1993 with the following cast:

Characters in order of appearance:

GERARD MCKINNON	Paul Higgins
JUDGE	Roger Swaine
JUSTICE CUDDEFORD	Michael Bryant
SIR PETER EDGECOMBE QC	Richard Pasco
IRINA PLATT	Alphonsia Emmanuel
WOODY PEARSON	Adam Kotz
PO RAYMOND BECKETT	Oliver Ford Davies
PC SANDRA BINGHAM	Katrina Levon
KEITH MACHIN	Chris Gascoyne
SERGEANT LESTER SPEED	Paul Moriarty
PC DAVE LAWRENCE	Edward Clayton
PC TOBY METCALFE	Adrian Scarborough
WOMAN UNDER ARREST	Judith Coke
ACCOMPLICE	Judy Damas

DC BARRY HOPPER	Mark Strong
DC ABDUL 'JIMMY' KHAN	Paul Bhattacharjee
PC ESTHER BALLY	Tacye Nichols
TOASTMASTER	Doyne Byrd
CHARLES KENDRICK MP	Nicholas Day
WAITRESS	Pamela Nomvete
BANGLADESHI MAN	Chook Sibtain
JASON	Tyrone Huggins
NELSON	Robert Tunstall
FIRST PRISONER	Paul Gilmore
SECOND PRISONER	Femi Elufowoju Jnr.
KEYBOARDS	Terry Davies

ACT ONE

ACT TWO

AUTHOR'S NOTE

I was helped in the writing of this play by the special kindness
and patience of many people from the police force, the bar, the
bench and the prison service. I welcome this chance to thank
them all. Faults of understanding are mine alone.

Murmuring Judges is the second play in a trilogy about
British institutions. The title of this play is from a legal
expression, meaning to speak ill of the judiciary. It is still an
offence in Scottish law.

So long as a judge keeps silent,
his reputation for wisdom and impartiality remains
unassailable.

Lord Chancellor Kilmuir

Professional people have no cares
Whatever happens they get theirs

Ogden Nash

ACT ONE

SCENE ONE

An empty stage. Then suddenly from nowhere they're all there – the judge, the jury, the battery of lawyers in wigs, the public, the police, the press, the ushers, the guards, and at the centre of the forward-facing court, the defendants. The entire company of the law has appeared in the blinking of an eye.

At the centre, the three defendants of whom GERARD MCKINNON *is conspicuously the youngest, barely in his twenties, thin, wiry, tall, his dark hair down to his shoulders. Beside him, crop-haired, pale, in suits, two other defendants,* TRAVIS *and* FIELDING. *But the emphasis of the light is on* MCKINNON, *and before you're ready he begins to speak. He has an Irish accent.*

GERARD: I'm standing here, I'm thinking, oh God, it's coming, it *is* coming, it's finally happening, hold on, remember, this is happening to me. After it going so slowly, *slowly*, the standing, the waiting – God, is there anything in the world slower than a lawyer? – after all that, now suddenly, stop, hold on, suddenly it's going so fast . . .
(The lights change to favour the whole court as the USHER *calls to make everyone stand.)*

CLERK: Has the jury reached a verdict upon which you are all agreed?

JURYMAN: We have.

CLERK: Do you find the defendant James Arthur Travis guilty or not guilty?

JURYMAN: Guilty.

CLERK: Do you find the defendant Michael Fielding guilty or not guilty?

I

JURYMAN: Guilty.

CLERK: Do you find the defendant Gerard Thomas McKinnon guilty or not guilty?

(*A slight pause.*)

JURYMAN: Guilty.

(*The lights change again as* GERARD *struggles to interrupt.*)

GERARD: And I want to say, yes, hold on, just a moment, take me back, I did meet these men, yes, I did, but I thought at the time, part of me thought, this is stupid, I mean, I'm not *really* doing this, there's a part of me which isn't standing on this freezing pavement, thinking how did I get myself into this? So why is it now, only now, yes, *now*, why is everything finally real?

(*The lights change back to favour the court.*)

JUDGE: And now I will turn to the sentencing. Please, will the prisoners attend?

(*The lights focus on* GERARD, *his speech more insistent than ever.*)

GERARD: Finally I get it, yes, it *is* happening, these men, every one of them silver-haired, judicious, informed, they will go home to their wives, to wine in fine glasses and the gossip of the Bar, they will walk the streets and complain about their lives, and I . . . (*He stops. More insistently.*) And *I* . . .

(*The court is lit again.*)

JUDGE: For Travis, eight years and six years to run concurrently. For Fielding, eight years and six concurrently also. For McKinnon . . . (*A pause.*) Five years.

(*The lights change, as if* GERARD *were at last alone. He is quiet.*)

GERARD: And *I* . . . the stuff of their profession . . . I will go to my gaol.

2

SCENE TWO

*The court at once melds into the incoming scene, led by the defence
counsel, who walk from the court towards us. At the centre of the
action is* SIR PETER EDGECOMBE QC, *who is tall, thin, fastidious,
in his early sixties, with a slightly raffish appearance which
contradicts the precision of his speech.*

*The new scene is in the open area giving on to the High Court.
The Hall of the Court is a great vaulted Victorian building with
noticeboards for the day's hearings. It is ten to two. The courts are
about to resume. A massive perspective is given to the area by
groups of lawyers and clients consulting before the courts'
resumptions.*

At the very front, MR JUSTICE CUDDEFORD *is coming along a
corridor on his way to work. He is in his early sixties, a large, bald
man, heavily built, incisive. As soon as he sees* SIR PETER *he greets
him warmly.*

CUDDEFORD: Sir Peter!
SIR PETER: Judge!
 (*They smile contentedly.*)
CUDDEFORD: Are you looking crestfallen?
SIR PETER: Crestfallen? No.
CUDDEFORD: They were saying at luncheon you'd just lost
 your case at the Bailey.
SIR PETER: Good Lord, I'm astonished anyone mentioned it.
CUDDEFORD: But they did.
SIR PETER: It was a very trivial affair. (*He smiles, unruffled.*) I
 only took a criminal case as a favour. Fair dos, Desmond.
 I came to it late.
CUDDEFORD: They all count. It spoils your bowling average.
SIR PETER: Hardly. Beaky Harris was meant to be leading the
 defence.
 (CUDDEFORD *smiles, as if we all know Beaky.*)
 But his horse was running in Paris. And I owed him one.
 It turned out to be a silly sort of warehouse robbery. And

3

Beaky didn't leave me much of a case.

(*He smiles.* IRINA PLATT *is standing one dutiful pace behind her silk. She is black, in her mid-twenties, neat, well presented, open-faced, with a quiet politeness which is hard to interpret.*)

CUDDEFORD: I was hoping to run into you. Because I heard you yesterday.

SIR PETER: Yesterday?

CUDDEFORD: I don't mean in court.

SIR PETER: Oh, I see. (*He smoothly introduces* IRINA.) You haven't met our new tenant?

CUDDEFORD: No.

SIR PETER: She's just joined our chambers. She was a Commonwealth scholar. Irina Platt. Mr Justice Cuddeford.

CUDDEFORD: Excellent.

IRINA: How do you do?

(CUDDEFORD *smiles slyly at* SIR PETER.)

CUDDEFORD: We were just discussing Sir Peter's latest public manifestation.

IRINA: Oh, yes.

CUDDEFORD: You heard it?

IRINA: I did.

SIR PETER: I do sometimes think it's the last remaining thing the British all hold in common. It's the only time we're really one nation.

CUDDEFORD: It's true.

SIR PETER: Just for that moment, Desmond, with all our differences, all our different attitudes to life, nevertheless, before Sunday luncheon, the whole nation stops and comes together.

CUDDEFORD: Yes, yes, I agree.

(SIR PETER *smiles modestly.*)

SIR PETER: It's extraordinary. Everyone listens to *Desert Island Discs*.

(IRINA *looks down, impassive.*)

4

CUDDEFORD: I liked the Brahms.

SIR PETER: Yes, I was saying to Irina at the Bailey this
morning, I accepted to do it not in any way for
myself . . .

CUDDEFORD: No.

SIR PETER: I had no personal motive at all. It's pure chance
I've featured in a few eye-catching cases . . .

CUDDEFORD: Indeed.

SIR PETER: So for that reason my name is known. I wanted to
speak on the programme on behalf of the whole
profession at large.

(CUDDEFORD *looks at him a moment*.)

CUDDEFORD: I see.

SIR PETER: Not least at this moment. People have such
forbidding ideas of our character. It seemed to me not
bad to show there is another side. (*He smiles*.) More
human, perhaps. More fallible, even.

CUDDEFORD: Yes. (*He frowns thoughtfully*.) I'm not sure your
records quite reflected that aim.

SIR PETER: What do you mean?

CUDDEFORD: Edith Piaf. If 'fallible' is how you wished to
appear . . . It's none of my business . . .

SIR PETER: Please . . .

CUDDEFORD: Maybe 'Non, je ne regrette rien' didn't quite hit
the mark.

(SIR PETER *turns to* IRINA, *about to defend himself, but*
CUDDEFORD *rides over him*.)

SIR PETER: Well . . .

CUDDEFORD: I admit it came out of a discussion of your
private life.

SIR PETER: Yes. I couldn't stop that.

CUDDEFORD: Why should you? A whistle-stop tour of your
wives. It was nice to catch up, so to speak. But I admit
to one ugly moment. I thought, oh my goodness, he's
out of control. But I misjudged you. You spared us 'My
Way'.

5

(SIR PETER *is a little discomforted by this in front of* IRINA.)

SIR PETER: The Piaf meant nothing, Desmond. I just like her voice.

(CUDDEFORD *looks confidently at* IRINA, *enjoying himself*.)

CUDDEFORD: Miss Platt, please ignore these old battles between us. It's probably jealousy. Peter and I started at the same time.

(*They are both smiling now*.)

SIR PETER: We regard Irina as a catch.

CUDDEFORD: I see that.

SIR PETER: She seemed to us to have all the assets we need in a forward-looking Bar.

CUDDEFORD: Yes. I see those. Most clearly.

SIR PETER: She was the unanimous choice. Of the whole of chambers. We all felt she is exactly the kind of person the Bar is now most eager to attract.

CUDDEFORD: Yes.

(*He smiles at* IRINA, *who has been quite still through all this, looking down*.)

SIR PETER: Mind you, the first day we had a bit of a problem. May I tell this story?

IRINA: Yes.

SIR PETER: Irina turned up to court in a rather brilliant green dress.

CUDDEFORD: Green? Oh, my goodness.

(*Both men smile, a shared pleasure in this*.)

I suppose everyone told you what old Chugger used to do?

IRINA: No.

SIR PETER: Chugger was a famous old judge.

CUDDEFORD: He'd say to a lady barrister, 'I'm sorry, I can't hear you.' She'd start speaking louder. 'I still can't hear you.' She'd say, 'Do you have a problem with my diction, my Lord?' 'No, I don't think so,' he'd say. 'I just sense I'd hear you more clearly if you attended the court wearing black.' (*He wheezes with laughter*.) Outrageous!

SIR PETER: Yes.

6

CUDDEFORD: Absolutely outrageous.
(IRINA *frowns slightly*.)
IRINA: But they still don't like it.
CUDDEFORD: Well, no.
IRINA: Sir Peter suggested I change.
CUDDEFORD: Yes. There is a serious point, I'm afraid. It's the
judge's court. It's his. He runs it as he sees fit. And, in
English law, it's very important he does.
(CUDDEFORD *is pleased with this, but* IRINA *is impassive,
her own view hidden*.)
SIR PETER: Irina has been doing her bit for all our freedoms.
CUDDEFORD: Oh, really?
SIR PETER: Yes. I've sent her out collecting for our Bar
Council fund.
CUDDEFORD: I heard rumour of a fund.
SIR PETER: We've decided to employ a well-known firm of
public-relations consultants.
CUDDEFORD: Public relations?
SIR PETER: People need to understand just what a threat to
justice the new legislation might be.
(CUDDEFORD *just looks at him a moment*.)
If we were to merge the functions of barrister and
solicitor, if any move were made to dismantle the
specialist Bar, I don't think the public begin to appreciate
just how disastrous the consequences would be.
CUDDEFORD: No.
SIR PETER: We started fund-raising for a campaign about four
days ago.
CUDDEFORD: How much have you raised?
IRINA: One million.
(*There is a sudden silence.* CUDDEFORD *turns and looks at
her*.)
CUDDEFORD: That sounds an auspicious start. One million?
SIR PETER: As you say.
IRINA: Give or take a few thousand.
CUDDEFORD: Well, well.

7

(IRINA's *gaze does not waver from* CUDDEFORD. *He is thoughtful.*)

Has anyone refused?

IRINA: No. No one.

CUDDEFORD: Remarkable.

SIR PETER: Yes. I think it underlines the profound depth of feeling. What did the Lord Chief say? 'Tyranny does not always arrive with a toothbrush moustache and wearing a swastika.'

CUDDEFORD: He did say that.

SIR PETER: Yes. (*He turns, at ease again now, on familiar ground.*) I can see, of course, the whole operation may seem vulgar. It may at first seem crass from people like us. That we should argue our case in the marketplace. But this is not entirely self-interested, Desmond. We act for all those who value professional life. (*He smiles in anticipation of his next, mischievous thought.*) And when some ... shady Tory politician is accused of consorting with some doxy behind Paddington Station, at that moment when he reaches for his telephone and says, 'Get me an expert, get me the finest specialist forensic advocate in the land', then at that point ... when he needs us ... then he will know the folly of diluting our profession. He will feel it, oh yes, most urgently. As urgently as if there were no electric light. (*He looks at them, his performance suspended before its coda.*) But until then, Desmond, the duty falls to us, I would say, to protect these politicians from their own worst instincts. (*He nods to himself.*) And I don't know anyone who doesn't see it that way.

(CUDDEFORD *smiles, quietly amused by this speech.*)

CUDDEFORD: You will work with this man?

IRINA: Yes.

CUDDEFORD: You are fortunate. You impress me, Peter. As always. *Quod erat demonstrandum.* (*He pauses, watchful.*) I would enter only one caveat, perhaps.

SIR PETER: What's that?

8

CUDDEFORD: The sum of money which Miss Platt has collected. (*He leans in a moment.*) Keep that to yourself. Why don't you? (*He smiles.*) *Verb. sap.* If the whole world is now to be public relations. Play down the million, Sir Peter.

(*Immediately beside him the* CLERK *of his court has appeared, gowned and respectful. The Hall behind has emptied out and there is a sudden hush now.*)

CLERK: Sir, the court is ready for you.

CUDDEFORD: Good. (*He turns to them.*) I must go and do some judging.

SIR PETER and IRINA: Judge.

(*There is a formality now, and* IRINA *even bows slightly.*)

CUDDEFORD: I trust I'll see you again.

(*He turns and goes.* IRINA *and* SIR PETER *stand a moment, etched in the light from the high windows. Then they part, going separate ways, and the stage lightens.*)

SCENE THREE

IRINA *turns from the courts, leaving* SIR PETER *to go in, and with her papers tucked under her arm sets off towards the Inns of Court. It's a fine sunny day, and she strides confidently across. As she does, she is joined by* WOODY PEARSON, *who is in his thirties, pencil-thin, clever, in a grey suit. He has a cockney accent. They head together towards Sir Peter's chambers.*

WOODY: Miss Platt, there you are.

IRINA: Woody, good afternoon.

WOODY: I heard this morning's turned out to be a pile of piss.

(*She hands him back the brief.*)

IRINA: It wasn't a great case.

WOODY: Yeah. I thought Beaky made a pretty smart move. He has this sort of allergy. When he hears the words 'legal aid'.

9

IRINA: I see. His horse wasn't running?

WOODY: How shall we know?

(*They have arrived at the chambers and gone into the outer office.* WOODY *starts sorting out briefs, which he hands to her.*)

This has just come in. You're in Kingston in the morning. Defending an ABH. All right? Then I hope we're going to get you over to Southwark. It's just for an adjournment. Have you got a car?

IRINA: Sure.

WOODY: How fast is it? Can you squeeze in a quick plea in Brighton? You can read it while you're driving.

(IRINA *smiles at him ironically.*)

IRINA: What about the interim injunction?

WOODY: Oh yeah, that's Thursday. But Sir Peter says he wants you both to work on it tonight.

IRINA: 'Sir Peter says'?

WOODY: Yeah.

IRINA: (*Frowns*) I was just with him at the High Court.

WOODY: You're to go and take in a little Mozart, he said. Then you'll work on here afterwards.

(IRINA *stops a moment, frowning.*)

IRINA: Woody, he could have just said.

WOODY: But he doesn't have to, does he? That's what he has me for.

IRINA: There's a word for what he's asking you to do.

WOODY: Yeah. 'Clerking'.

IRINA: Is that what it's called?

(*They both smile. It's easy-going between them, but* WOODY *is behaving as if this were all quite usual.*)

WOODY: Don't fret. It's only for appearances. He goes to Covent Garden, he needs something nice to hold his right arm. To be *seen* to hold his right arm. (*He throws a quick glance at her.*) Ease up. It happens.

IRINA: If you're the intermediary, tell him the answer is no.

(*He is not thrown for a second.*)

10

WOODY: No? OK. I'll write that down, so I don't get it wrong. Just remind me: opera, invitation, message from the new girl, sorry, afraid she won't go.

IRINA: I didn't say sorry.

WOODY: No. I invented that. It must have been the last one.

IRINA: What do you mean?

WOODY: The last new girl we had here. Very bright. From Harvard. I was told she was an absolute whiz with her torts. She said no. As I recall, to Wagner. Well, fair enough. I avoid anything where people sing in helmets. (*He looks at* IRINA. *Then, softly*) But look at it the other way. Where is she now?

(IRINA *doesn't respond.* WOODY *moves round nearer her.*) Miss Platt. If you work in the law, there's a lot of big issues. There are moments when you need people's help. It's quite plain, you're pretty feisty. The time is going to come when you want to make a stand. About something. I don't know what. (*He pauses, suddenly quiet and serious for the first time.*) Don't waste it on something which really doesn't matter. Like whether you're in the Crush Bar tonight. Why put his back up? Why start badly? He's innocent. He's a decent man. He's flash but he's decent. It's good advice. Fight when it matters. Because, surely to God, that moment will come.

(IRINA *is watching him closely, hearing all this. But then she shakes her head.*)

IRINA: I'm saying no. It's beginning wrong. It's the wrong start.

(*He thinks a moment, looking down, still gentle.*)

WOODY: You see, the thing is, Irina, the point is, it's a team. There's a lot of latitude. But you play in a team. You want to start inside, not outside.

IRINA: I know that. (*She smiles at him, touched by his genuine concern.*) Thank you, Woody. (*She turns and goes into her office.*) And now I have to get back to work.

11

SCENE FOUR

*The stage darkens and we move into the enormous, gloomy space of
the prison reception area. The prison is Victorian, with a gigantic
door just discernible at the back. It is late night, with only a few
high lights making shapes through the gloom. What by day is a busy
area with a very long desk running along one side is now deserted
and quiet.* RAYMOND BECKETT, *in his fifties, large, balding, with
a big stomach beneath his blue pullover, and an open, blunt
manner, is waiting behind the desk.*

At once from the back GERARD *is escorted out of the darkness by
a short, foxy-looking* OFFICER *who brings him in to face*
BECKETT.

BECKETT: Strip off.

GERARD: I'm sorry?

BECKETT: Empty all your pockets and take off your clothes.
(GERARD *looks, a little bewildered, round the huge space. The
other* OFFICER *has already disappeared into the darkness at
the other side of the area.*)

GERARD: Here?
(BECKETT *looks up from the admission sheets, catching*
GERARD's *tone.*)

BECKETT: Don't you know the procedures? Haven't you been
in prison before?

GERARD: No.

BECKETT: Weren't you on remand?

GERARD: I was on bail.

BECKETT: So is this your first time?
(GERARD *looks at him, not needing to answer.* BECKETT
seems to show a sudden sympathy. The other OFFICER *has
returned with a large cloth bag.*)
Why aren't you emptying your pockets?
(GERARD *moves to the desk and empties his pockets on to it.*
BECKETT *has a plastic bag, which he puts the stuff in.*)
Here. Your things will go in this bag.

(GERARD *starts to undress. The silent* OFFICER *has started to empty what looks like a pile of rags onto a table opposite.*)

BECKETT: Why are you so late?

GERARD: They took me to Pentonville. But then it turned out there wasn't any room.

BECKETT: There's no room here. But we'll make some. Why is it midnight?

GERARD: Then there wasn't a van.

BECKETT: Again?

GERARD: They couldn't find one.

BECKETT: Have you eaten?

GERARD: I had some spaghetti. But then I lost it.

BECKETT: How are you feeling?

GERARD: Not very well.

(BECKETT *is filling out forms. The other* OFFICER, *non-committal, now goes to lean against a desk a long way off. He lights a cigarette, says nothing, just watches.*)

BECKETT: We've put you on D-wing. We shouldn't really. It's for lifers. But it's that or sleeping in the chapel.

(*There is a sudden silence.* GERARD *is in the middle of the area, covering his nakedness with his hand. His clothes are in a pile beside him.* BECKETT *holds out the form on a clipboard to the naked man.*)

Sign here.

GERARD: I can't. You've taken my pen.

(BECKETT *looks at him a moment, not sure if* GERARD *is taking the piss.* GERARD *signs.*)

BECKETT: Would you like a cigarette?

GERARD: No, thank you.

BECKETT: You're meant to have a shower. But the water's off. So you can get dressed.

GERARD: I'm sorry?

BECKETT: There's clothes over there.

(*He points towards the heap.* GERARD *goes over and collects his prison clothes.*)

Gerard McKinnon.

13

GERARD: Yes.

BECKETT: I'm giving you a number. All right? A6324. That's what you'll answer to. Do you need to hear it again?

GERARD: No, I've got it.

BECKETT: The governor will come and see you in the morning. And we'll fix you with a job. Prison isn't just sitting around.

GERARD: No. (*He is frowning at the outsize tops and trousers, while at the same time trying to stay decent.*) No, I know that.

BECKETT: You'll see all the departments. There's a reception committee. Probation, medical, educational, the chaplain. They'll advise you on how to survive in the gaol.

GERARD: Survive?

BECKETT: Just so you don't waste your time. It's up to you. You can make this place work for you. Anyone can. It's not hard. Get educated. Be sensible.

GERARD: Yes. (*He stops a moment, hesitating to speak, halfway dressed.*) It's silly, you see, I was sent down with two other people. I was expecting they'd be here with me.

BECKETT: That's not the policy.

GERARD: No. I'm not complaining. I don't like them that much. It's just . . . they're more experienced. So I thought they might sort of see me through.

BECKETT: Yeah. (*He is looking hard at* GERARD.) Look, I think someone better tell you. Before you get started. You'd better learn. I've seen people go crazy when it's their first time. (*He pauses.*) What you have to do is put the past behind you. Do you understand?
(GERARD *frowns a moment, as he dresses.*)
You got done. You did wrong. Society's put you in gaol. OK, now don't brood. Work to the future. Work to the moment when you get out.

GERARD: Yes, I see.

BECKETT: Because you know what's most dangerous?

GERARD: No, I don't.

14

BECKETT: The worst is getting bitter. That's the thing. I watch it. That's the thing that messes people up. Do you see? If you get an attitude. If you get an attitude, I tell you, it's worse than catching the clap. (*He suddenly raises his voice across the area, without warning.*) An attitude's the clap. Do you understand me?

GERARD: What sort of attitude?

BECKETT: If you start thinking, they done me wrong, I'm always in the right, I hate this place, I shouldn't be here, and, pardon my French, sod you all, if you think that, then it kills you. You're finished. It burns you up.

GERARD: Yes. (*He looks at* BECKETT *nervously.*) I'll tell you what worries me.

BECKETT: Yes?

GERARD: I got a wife.

BECKETT: OK.

GERARD: She's not my wife actually. But we have two children. One of them has Down's.

BECKETT: Yes. Go on.

GERARD: Down's syndrome, you see. (*He pauses, emotion about to overwhelm him for a moment.*) And I'm not sure how they'll keep their heads above water.

(*He stands a moment, the clothes ridiculously big for him.*)

BECKETT: Right, well, that's it, that's what I'm saying. There's some people here going to help you with that. There's people with degrees from Oxford University. They're giving up their lives to help you adjust. So you can live with being banged up.

(*He gets up now to go and pick up the old clothes which* GERARD *has discarded on the floor, and to put them in a bag.*) It's a long job. It's not always easy. It's not like changing your clothes.

(BECKETT *is now standing directly opposite* GERARD. *His original clothes are in a plastic bag, while he is like Charlie Chaplin, his trousers puddling round his feet, his jacket swamping him.*)

15

GERARD: Do you have a belt?

BECKETT: You're not allowed a belt. You'll kill yourself. (*He nods a moment.*) Do you want a cup of tea?

GERARD: I won't, thank you.

(*There's a moment's pause, things oddly formal and polite.*) I'd like to sleep.

BECKETT: Good. You look good.

GERARD: Thank you.

(BECKETT *looks to the other* OFFICER)

BECKETT: Shall we go up?

SCENE FIVE

Before they have gone, SANDRA BINGHAM *has appeared. She is in a uniform, a WPC, in her mid-twenties with neat, dyed-blond short hair. She is quite small and tidy. She speaks directly to us. As she does so, the gaol is replaced by the charge room of a large inner-London police station. A long desk dominates the room, and opposite it is a self-locking door, which gives on to the outside world. To one side of the long room is a passage which leads to the cells; to the other, the front desk of the police station.*

You are aware of the activity in the room behind as SANDRA *speaks to us, but the emphasis of the light is on her.*

SANDRA: You see, it's all mess. That's what it is, mostly. If you take the charge room for instance, there's maybe thirty or forty people arrested in a day. Most of them are people who simply can't cope. They've been arrested before – petty thieving, deception, stealing car radios, selling stolen credit cards in pubs. Or not even that. Disturbing the peace. Failing to appear on a summons. Failing to carry out conditions of bail. Failing to produce a current car licence. Failing to fulfil Community Service. Getting drunk. Getting drunk and going for a joyride. Getting drunk and then driving home. Attacking your wife. Who

16

then won't testify. Trying to cash a stolen cheque, only being so stupid you don't even try to make the signatures match. Opening telephone boxes. Fifty–fifty fights in clubs which are nobody's fault. Crimes of opportunity. Not being able to resist it. Then going back, thinking I got away with it last time. Possession. One acid tab. One Ninja Turtle sticker containing LSD. One smoke. One sniff. One toke. One three-quid packet. (*She smiles.*) That's the basic stuff. It's the stuff of policing. All you have to do with it is be a ledger clerk. You fill in bits of paper. Every officer carries thirty-six bits of paper about their person at any one time.

(SANDRA *starts to move round the room to collect the boy she has just arrested. She stops a moment, before the scene begins.*) Policing's largely the fine art of getting through biros. And keeping yourself ready for the interesting bits.

(*At once the lights change and the scene begins with* SANDRA *coming through the door that leads to the outside world with an obstreperous seventeen-year-old boy who is in a touchy and aggressive mood.* KEITH *is in a blouson, and light cotton jeans, surprisingly slight for someone who looks ready to pick a fight with anyone. At the desk* SERGEANT LESTER SPEED *is sitting, filling out forms. He is in his late thirties, with a loud voice, powerful, heavily built. He effortlessly dominates the room. A smart, young, dark-haired policewoman,* ESTHER BALLY, *is busy behind him.*)

KEITH: I didn't bloody do it. Don't bloody touch me.

SANDRA: What is this?

(*She lets* KEITH *go, affronted by his behaviour. He makes several feints, lifting his arms as if to protect himself from being handled again.*)

KEITH: Leave me. Just leave me.

SANDRA: I'm not touching you.

KEITH: Leave me.

SANDRA: I'm not touching you, all right?

(KEITH *moves away, standing right up against the wall,*

17

cowering, twenty feet from SANDRA. LESTER *just watches*.)

KEITH: Don't bloody touch me.

SANDRA: I'm not bloody touching you.

LESTER: Good morning, Sandra.

SANDRA: Nice to see you, Sergeant.

(*She turns to* KEITH. *There is a moment's stalemate*.)
This is your custody officer. It's his job to tell you your rights.

(LESTER *reaches down to get out the appropriate form from his desk*.)

LESTER: I need a 57.

KEITH: I'm not saying anything.

LESTER: Sit down.

KEITH: I'm not sitting down.

LESTER: You'll have to sit eventually.

KEITH: You're a bloody pig.

LESTER: That's right. You're very observant. (*He has started filling in the form*.) God, have you had this all the way here?

SANDRA: Yes, I have, Sarge.

LESTER: You should be chuffed. Sandra's one of our high-flyers. It's very rare Sandra's not got her head in her books. Isn't that right?

SANDRA: Absolutely right.

(LESTER *smiles to himself as he writes*.)

LESTER: She's in the fast lane. You should be flattered she's brought in a body at all. Let alone *you*. Name?

KEITH: I'm not saying anything.

LESTER: Then don't.

KEITH: I don't want to be here.

LESTER: I don't want to be here either. I want to be in bed with Michelle Pfeiffer. But what we're talking about is what's called reality. Name?

(*Wordlessly*, KEITH *climbs on to the bench and stands on top of it*. LESTER *takes no notice*.)
Right. No name at present. Thank you, Sandra, now the rundown on the arrest.

(SANDRA *is opposite* LESTER, *also ignoring* KEITH.)

SANDRA: I was in Redwood Road. I saw this young man, leaning against a car, applying pressure to the handle. When he saw me, he started to run . . .

LESTER: OK . . .

SANDRA: I caught up, I got hold of him, I told him I was authorized to search his pockets . . . I found this.

(*She puts a small brown lump down on the desk.* LESTER *at once reaches down to another drawer to get a plastic bag and seal it.*)

And that's a small piece of what I think is dope.

KEITH: She bloody put it on me.

LESTER: Oh, you're talking.

KEITH: She put it in my pocket.

(LESTER *breaks off from writing, looks up, smiling slightly.*)

LESTER: I wouldn't say that, if I were you.

KEITH: Why the hell not?

LESTER: Because if you make an allegation against an officer, it's very serious. I have to fill in a completely different form. *And I've started this one.* (*He smiles.*) Do you get my point? Do you get what I mean?

(*At once through the door comes a fresh group: two women guided by two thickly clad policemen. The older* WOMAN *is in her forties, in a pink velour jumpsuit. The younger one looks like her* DAUGHTER.)

Oh God, it looks like crime's back in fashion again.

(*The older of the two policemen is* DAVE LAWRENCE, *a jug-eared Welshman, stubby, in his fifties. He is putting the* WOMAN's *handbag and purse on the desk, while she is guided to the desk by* TOBY METCALFE, *an almost embarrassingly young, fair-haired Yorkshire boy.* SANDRA *meanwhile sits down on the other side of the desk, writing her notes.*)

DAVE: I brought this couple in, Sarge. I was called along by Sainsbury's. It's on suspicion of chequebook fraud.

LESTER: All right, they'll have to wait, there's a queue.

WOMAN: I'm not sitting there.

19

(LESTER *waves airily at* KEITH *who is still standing on the bench.*)

LESTER: Please, go and stand up there next to him, it makes no difference to me.

WOMAN: I don't like the look of it.

DAVE: Esther, can you do a quick frisk?

(*The* DAUGHTER *has begun to cry.*)

WOMAN: She's not feeling well.

LESTER: No, well, I'm not feeling wonderful.

(*The* WOMAN *takes her* DAUGHTER *in her arms.*)

DAVE: You all right, my love?

WOMAN: She had cancer, you see.

LESTER: Uh-huh. (*He pauses a moment, uncharacteristically lost for words. Then, to divert, turns to* TOBY.) You all right?

TOBY: Me? Fine. (*He frowns.*) I'm fine, Sarge.

LESTER: So, who's going to do the report?

TOBY: Oh, well . . .

DAVE: You get some practice, Toby.

(DAVE *and* ESTHER *are attending to the* WOMEN *while* TOBY *goes to the desk to make the formal report.*)

TOBY: Well, we were called in by the check-out manager at Sainsbury's. Look at these – you see the signatures don't match. Here, their real names are on their family-supplement books. And so . . . well, we made a joint decision, me and Dave.

LESTER: Astonishing. Unaided?

TOBY: We felt we had grounds to bring them in.

(LESTER *nods and raises his voice.*)

LESTER: You're being detained. Do you understand what's happening?

WOMAN: Of course. I'm not stupid.

LESTER: Is she all right now?

WOMAN: She's OK.

LESTER: I'm reading you your rights. Do you want a solicitor?

(*The* WOMEN *look at one another uncertainly.*)

We'll get you the duty one.

20

ESTHER: What's happening with the frisking?

DAVE: Nothing. It's abandoned.

(DAVE *shakes his head.* LESTER *is holding out two forms for them.*)

LESTER: Sign. Your real name.

(*As the* WOMEN *move across to sign,* LESTER *turns to* ESTHER.)

Can you call that solicitor?

ESTHER: Sure.

LESTER: Abu ben Dhabi, or whatever he's called. (*He keeps pointing the* WOMEN *to other places to sign.*) And here. He's of the Asian persuasion.

DAVE: Nothing wrong with that.

LESTER: 'Course you'd say that. Because you're a bloody Taffy.

DAVE: I am. And proud of it.

LESTER: Oh yeah? All you bloody nationalists. If you're so proud of it, why d'you drive up the M4 every ten days?

DAVE: Because the money's better.

LESTER: OK. You're culturally dependent, mate. And don't you forget it.

DAVE: Don't think there's much chance of that.

(*He takes back the forms.*)

LESTER: Thank you. Now please – I'm sorry this is all we have. Our hospitality suite. You might as well use it. I think you're going to have a long wait.

(*Now from the front desk of the station come two plainclothes men, both holding plastic cups.* BARRY HOPPER *is in his mid-thirties, cheerful, outgoing, wearing thick dark glasses, like a film star. Beside him is* ABDUL KHAN, *known as* JIMMY, *spry, lightweight beside* BARRY, *and a real snappy dresser.*)

BARRY: Good morning, all.

DAVE: Oh God, here they come. Wreathed in garlands.

(BARRY *makes a mock bow to the room, then stands practising his golf swing.*)

21

BARRY: Just talented. Me and my partner. Just supremely talented. If you have any problems please do call CID.

LESTER: I thought you'd be on a bloody chariot today.

BARRY: Take no notice, Jimmy.

JIMMY: I shan't.

BARRY: It's simple jealousy. Yes, we did manage rather a big case, since you ask.

JIMMY: Nothing to it.

DAVE: Yeah. Did you see the carpenters?

BARRY: What carpenters?

LESTER: They're widening all the doors.

DAVE: Yeah. To get Barry's head through.

(LESTER *looks admiringly at* JIMMY'*s suit*.)

LESTER: I like the whistle, Jimmy.

JIMMY: Well, thank you.

LESTER: If I was a shit-hot detective, do you think they'd let me dress up like that?

JIMMY: Not in your case, Lester. You do need the body as well.

(DAVE *grins at this*.)

LESTER: Got a hangover, Barry? The glasses are good.

BARRY: My eyes are swimming behind them.

LESTER: Big party, was it?

(BARRY *has leant right over the back of* LESTER'*s chair, after a lap of the room, and while talking is examining the neat line of sheets that are laid out on top of the desk in front of* LESTER.)

BARRY: It's like a small rodent has pissed in my mouth.

(*Everyone is working now, just ignoring the suspects.* DAVE *is rifling through the woman's handbag.* LESTER *is filling in forms.* JIMMY *has picked up the substance bag and is holding it up inquiringly*.)

DAVE: Yes, well, it's possible. In the position you were in when I last saw you.

LESTER: Horizontal, was he?

BARRY: I was conducting an interview.

DAVE: Yeah. We saw. With the barmaid.

22

(BARRY *smiles across at* JIMMY.)

BARRY: Take no notice, Jimmy. English sense of humour.

(SANDRA *has moved across beside* JIMMY. BARRY *takes his glasses off as she comes into his eyeline.*)

SANDRA: Will you take a look at this, Jimmy?

BARRY: Oh, it's you.

SANDRA: Good morning, Barry.

BARRY: I didn't see you.

SANDRA: No. (*She smiles and goes back to work.*) Well, I'm here.

(*The atmosphere changes subtly as* BARRY *goes back to examining the day's work.*)

BARRY: So what do we have?

JIMMY: Whose is it?

SANDRA: Belongs to him.

LESTER: Sandra's brought in this body. Invoking his right to silence.

BARRY: That's good. It's your democratic right. That's what it's for. You use it.

LESTER: But there's a major procedural problem.

(JIMMY *has thrown the pack across the room to* BARRY, *who holds it up to look at it.*)

BARRY: Oh! Illegal substances.

LESTER: I can't fill in the form because he won't tell me his name.

KEITH: I'm not bloody talking. You're all bloody bastards.

(BARRY *looks at him a moment, then nods to* JIMMY.)

BARRY: I see. All right, get some tapes, will you, Jimmy?

JIMMY: Happy to.

BARRY: Because we have to interview you on tape, that's the law of the land.

(JIMMY *goes to the drawer and gets tapes which* LESTER *inspects and signs out.*)

KEITH: If you bloody touch me, I'll have you. I'll get you for wrongful arrest.

(BARRY *is moving towards him, nodding.*)

23

JIMMY: Do you want a solicitor?

KEITH: I'm not saying anything.

JIMMY: What do you think, Lester, can we take that as no?

(BARRY *stands a moment, looking up beneath the boy. Then he turns back and points at the* WOMAN.)

BARRY: All right, fair enough, we can do these two first.

(*The others laugh as* SANDRA *at once protests.*)

SANDRA: Oh, hang around, just wait a moment . . .

BARRY: All right . . .

SANDRA: I never understand it. You make an arrest, it takes precisely two minutes, you bring them in and you wait, on average, on *average*, four hours, that's half your relief . . .

LESTER: Yeah, yeah, we know it . . .

BARRY: Well, you know the answer.

DAVE: We all do.

BARRY: It's simple.

(*Suddenly all the police, familiar with the problem, join in a chant.*)

ALL: *Don't bring anyone in.*

(BARRY *smiles triumphantly round the room.*)

BARRY: I mean, come on, you boys, just think of it, if you never made any arrests, you'd all be out there on the streets all the time, and London would be so much better policed.

(*He sits down right by the bench on which the* WOMEN *have now sat.*)

So what are we going to do? I don't know. I suppose we're going to sit here.

(*The* DAUGHTER *is beginning to cry again.* BARRY *ignores* KEITH *above him, on the other side.*)

Good morning, madam. I'm Barry. How are you?

WOMAN: All right.

BARRY: Well, good. Do I know you? Haven't you used us before?

WOMAN: Once or twice.

BARRY: I thought I'd seen you. (*To the* DAUGHTER.) Would you

24

like a cup of coffee?

WOMAN: She wouldn't mind something to eat.

BARRY: Lester?

LESTER: Sure.

(BARRY *looks up at* KEITH.)

BARRY: Sunshine? What about you?

(KEITH *doesn't answer.* DAVE *has checked through the handbag and is trying to give the credit cards to* LESTER.)

LESTER: Has someone nicked the light-meal vouchers?

DAVE: At least we can do these. Can we do a check for stolen numbers?

LESTER: Ah, you're in luck, *main*-meal vouchers! They'll just have to do . . .

(*The* WOMAN *looks round. It is quietly industrious and cheerful.* BARRY *has a grin on his face, as if this hiatus is perfectly enjoyable.*)

WOMAN: Why are you lot so cheerful?

LESTER: Why are we cheerful? We're cheerful because Barry here had a bit of luck.

BARRY: What do you mean, 'luck'? (*He turns scornfully to the* WOMAN.) Don't believe it, darling. It wasn't luck.

DAVE: You see, he's a detective. And he finally managed to detect.

BARRY: Now that is a travesty. Here, ask Jimmy.

JIMMY: I'm not getting into this.

LESTER: Oh, Barry's getting shirty.

BARRY: I bloody well am.

LESTER: CID hates it when you call it luck. In uniform, you see, we don't mind admitting. We're sort of *grown-up* in that way.

BARRY: (*More insistent*) It wasn't luck.

(LESTER *is laughing as he writes.*)

LESTER: This is Barry's big triumph. Yesterday he and Jimmy were at the Bailey – all right? – they got three pretty nasty villains put away. Only what they don't tell you is how he found them in the first place.

25

BARRY: All right, you go on, I don't mind, you say what you like.
(*He waves a hand at* LESTER *to continue. The* WOMAN *frowns.*)
WOMAN: How did you find them?
DAVE: By brilliant detection.
BARRY: All right . . .
LESTER: Meaning: there was this woman who actually ran out into the street at two o'clock in the morning, finds the patrolling officer, who happens to be Sandra . . .
SANDRA: That's right.
LESTER: Who happens – by chance – to be driving right by, and she says there's a very loud party. It's a (*ironic stress*) 'celebration' or something in the council flat right next to hers. And she can't get to sleep because the music's too loud.
SANDRA: I go in . . .
LESTER: Yeah, and on the floor, oh my goodness, there she sees three leather coats, identical . . .
BARRY: All right . . .
LESTER: And – hey! – a toolbag. So, because she's quite bright, she leaves as if she's seen nothing, and goes and sits in her car. Sure enough, ten minutes later, they take the stuff down to a lock-up just behind the flat. (*He looks ironically at* BARRY.) So next morning, in goes Hercule Poirot. Into the lock-up where he finds two hundred leather coats, then into the flat, with about six of us. And being a detective doesn't look too bloody hard.
BARRY: I'm not telling any of you what happens after.
DAVE: Why not, Barry?
BARRY: How you make the connections. How you actually connect the right people to the job. How you make the case watertight. How you see it through to court.
DAVE: How is that done, Barry?
BARRY: Through what is called the exercise of my professional skill.

26

(*They all laugh.*)

LESTER: Oh yeah, right, thank you . . .

DAVE: Yeah. I think we saw that last night.

LESTER: What, you mean with the barmaid?

(BARRY *smiles contentedly and then looks up at* KEITH *above him.*)

BARRY: What do you think, lad? Are you listening to this?

(*There's suddenly a moment's pause in all the kidding. When* KEITH *speaks, he's quite serious.*)

KEITH: I tell you what I think. The police are all tossers. You'd have to be a tosser to want to do the job. Yeah.

BARRY: Yeah. You're right. That is probably true. (*He is wistful, as if now seriously considering it.*) Or rather, people call you a tosser. I mean, look at Lester. He sits opposite that door. People call him names, maybe twenty times a day. You'd have to be a tosser to be able to put up with it. At least without showing you mind.

(*He smiles.* SANDRA *has stopped work to listen, enjoying* BARRY's *line of thought.*)

Or perhaps you *don't* mind. Perhaps you stop minding. What would you say, Lester? After a while you find you've taken so much shit from people whingeing about how they hate the police, you just think fair enough . . . I'm not sure I care for the public that much.

(LESTER *says nothing, knowing what* BARRY *is up to.* BARRY *does not even look at* KEITH.)

Cuts both ways, doesn't it?

(*There is silence now in the charge room.*)

I'll tell you my idea of a tosser. He's someone who's been caught with a small piece of dope. The chances are he'll get off with a caution. Which if he had any nous he would know. But this one wants to get sent down for resisting arrest.

(*There's a pause.*)

KEITH: Did you say a caution?

BARRY: We haven't interviewed you yet. (*He is still not*

27

looking at KEITH.) Name?

KEITH: Keith Machin.

BARRY: Age?

KEITH: Seventeen.

(LESTER *writes*.)

LESTER: Did you say she planted this on you?

(KEITH *pauses a second*.)

KEITH: No.

LESTER: Do you want a solicitor?

KEITH: No.

LESTER: Then sign here.

(KEITH *gets down from the bench to sign.* BARRY *takes no notice, as if it were inevitable*.)

BARRY: You'll take him, will you, Jimmy?

JIMMY: I will.

SANDRA: Empty your pockets.

(*She begins to go through his things*.)

BARRY: What about these two?

LESTER: They're coming down with me. Get Esther, because we need to do a body search.

WOMAN: You're not looking up my whatsit.

LESTER: Madam, I most certainly am not. I wouldn't dream of abusing my position.

(*He has gathered a big bunch of keys, which he now takes off down the corridor, leading the two* WOMEN, DAVE *and* TOBY *away with him.* BARRY *has got up*.)

KEITH: You promised me a caution.

BARRY: I didn't promise you. I mentioned it, all right? Now, you get along and confess your heart out to Jimmy. (*He smiles*.) You can't shock Jimmy. He's very good with youth.

JIMMY: I am.

BARRY: He still gets on with yobs. All right, sunshine?

(*As a parting gesture,* KEITH *throws the pen on the floor, and goes out with* JIMMY. *Suddenly* BARRY *and* SANDRA *are almost alone*.)

28

He could be my son. That's what I think. When I see the young ones. Not that I'd ever know. I never see Rory. Not since his mother ran off with the antiques dealer from Cheltenham. (*He turns and smiles at her*.) I think she chose him to insult me.

SANDRA: No. That's just how it seems.

(*They both smile*.)

BARRY: How are you?

SANDRA: You seem well.

BARRY: Sure. I mean, it's a sort of a record. The Crown Prosecution Service didn't lose the papers. The witnesses actually turned up. There was no psychiatrist to say their mothers never gave them the tit. Three men were actually sent down for a crime they committed. (*He shakes his head*.) Heavens to Betsy, we got a result!

SANDRA: Well done.

BARRY: I watched you in the corridor. Outside the court, last day of the trial. Even there you were studying.

SANDRA: Naturally. I'm going on a course.

BARRY: Oh yes, I'm sure you are.

(*They both smile*.)

When you die, you know, there's a fork in the road with two pathways. One leads straight to heaven, that's where most people go. But to policemen they say, would you prefer the road marked 'Courses for *preparing* for heaven'? And do you know over half the coppers say yes?

(SANDRA *laughs. He has moved over and sat on the edge of the desk*.)

SANDRA: What you did just now, with the boy . . .

BARRY: Yeah?

SANDRA: It made me laugh. It was textbook.

BARRY: Sure.

SANDRA: Divert attention with some stories. Do everything you can to take the pressure off.

BARRY: That's right. Then you throw the golden bridge. I love it.

SANDRA: (*Quoting from memory*) 'The suspect must believe he has a means of escape.'

(BARRY *shrugs*.)

BARRY: Doesn't often work, I tell you.

SANDRA: You must be getting lucky.

BARRY: It's true. I'm on a streak. I'd been after that lot.

SANDRA: Did you know them?

BARRY: Sure. What, Travis and Fielding? Yes, of course I knew them. I know all the villains. As it happens I'd known them for years.

(SANDRA *frowns*.)

SANDRA: Then why didn't you say so?

BARRY: Didn't I?

(*She turns away, disbelieving*.)

SANDRA: Barry, you astonish me.

BARRY: Why?

SANDRA: Because when we all went in with the search warrant, you never gave the slightest sign you'd met them before.

BARRY: No. (*He shrugs, trying to turn it away*.) Well, there was no point. We knew they'd done a load of other jobs.

SANDRA: How did you know that?

BARRY: In the way you do. You just *know*. But because me and Jimmy'd never been able to stick those jobs on them, we decided to let them go by.

(SANDRA *is shaking her head*.)

SANDRA: You never even mentioned it. In all the time we were preparing the case.

BARRY: Didn't I? Oh really?

SANDRA: Did you know all of them?

BARRY: I knew Travis and Fielding.

SANDRA: That's what I mean. What about McKinnon?

BARRY: No. No, actually. McKinnon was new.

(*His tone is thoughtful for a moment, and* SANDRA *responds to the doubt in his voice*.)

SANDRA: I wasn't sure if he was guilty.

30

BARRY: Of course he was guilty. Forensic linked him to the stuff, and to the van.

SANDRA: He sat outside?

BARRY: Most likely. Yes. He was the driver, wasn't he?

SANDRA: And he wasn't there when the guard was tied up.

BARRY: No.

SANDRA: But he got five years.

BARRY: Yeah.

SANDRA: For a first offence? I suppose, I'm asking, did that surprise you?

BARRY: He lied. That didn't help him. Let's face it, he told a pack of lies. What's more, he was, sort of, well, what's the word? He was kind of *Irish* as well.
(*He smiles, but* SANDRA *pursues it.*)

SANDRA: He wasn't Irish, he's British.

BARRY: Oh, very funny. He may happen to hail from the North. But he did stand with a load of Micks outside the Irish pub on Clapham Common every evening. I think we can guess his primary allegiance.

SANDRA: And you think judges take that into account?
(BARRY *shakes his head.*)

BARRY: Oh, leave it out, Sandra, you're not just out of Hendon . . .

SANDRA: I'm asking.

BARRY: You're not in the Dream Palace now.

SANDRA: I'm not being stupid, I'm interested, you tell me . . . are you really saying that's how judges' minds work?
(BARRY *tries to be as firm as he can.*)

BARRY: Sandra, we are talking about a body of men who sometimes choose to go to work dressed in stockings and suspenders. I'm buggered if I know how their bloody minds work.

SANDRA: All right, all right . . .
(BARRY *is shaking his head, insistent.*)

BARRY: Darling, you do have to deal with that. I'm not being funny. Next time you're tempted to be serious when you

31

look at a judge. Under the robes. Under the language. Under the gravity. Please remember: he has made a style choice for which any adult male except Danny La Rue would be instantly arrested.

SANDRA: And is that why a man with an Irish accent gets such a bad deal?

(BARRY *looks at her, squaring with her now.*)

BARRY: All right, look, they don't *know* they're prejudiced. That's not how they think of it. It's like when I do an interview, I've never turned round and said, 'You black bastard.' But when I come out, I can't help it, I always feel virtuous because I *haven't* said it. It's like you've done them a favour. You actually start thinking, oh, I must be a really nice bloke. (*He nods.*) And that was my take on what happened yesterday. I know it. I've seen it so many times. The judge thought, I'm being nice, I'm being decent, I'm giving him less than the others. In *spite* of the fact that he's Irish.

SANDRA: He isn't. He isn't Irish.

BARRY: God, you're stubborn.

SANDRA: I know. (*She smiles, uneasy.*) It's just . . . you know . . . I did get a sight of him. I got a long look at this bloke.

BARRY: And? What?

(*She shakes her head, slightly embarrassed.*)

SANDRA: He's just a lad.

BARRY: That's none of our business.

SANDRA: He's got a very young family.

BARRY: So?

(SANDRA *shifts away.*)

So?

SANDRA: Look, I'm not green, I've always known what I was in for. Scrotes and dickheads. You know, I've told you my family's been full of police . . .

BARRY: Your Dad . . .

SANDRA: That's right. (*She looks at him a moment.*) I mean, yeah, my Dad for a start. So they always warned me. Fair

32

enough. I don't see things differently. They told me. You choose our profession, you spend your time with scrotes and dickheads all day. (*She pauses a second.*) But what do you do when you bring one in who isn't?

(BARRY *laughs.*)

BARRY: Oh, what, and the nice ones shouldn't go down?

SANDRA: No . . .

BARRY: There should be a sort of test? What, the niceness defence? Yes, your Honour, my client did do it, he did it, but you should see him, he's magic with children and animals. (*He turns away.*) Just lock 'em up, Sandra. We're not playing God.

(*She shakes her head, not taking him seriously.*)

SANDRA: Why do you pretend?

BARRY: Pretend?

SANDRA: Yes. Acting heartless.

BARRY: I'm not acting. I am.

SANDRA: You know that's not true.

BARRY: Isn't it?

SANDRA: No. No, it isn't. Not when we're alone.

BARRY: Oh, *well* . . . that's different.

(*They both smile.*)

SANDRA: Any more than you've ever looked at a barmaid in your life.

BARRY: Oh, that.

SANDRA: Yes.

(*She has moved away to a filing cabinet to catch up on her paperwork.* BARRY *is still on the desk, laughing now.*)

BARRY: Well, you have to do all that, don't you? If you're a copper, I mean. You've got to *be* a copper. It's expected. You have to give it lots of mouth. Talk about how you go over the side. If you say, oh, I just went home, had a Lucozade and thought about Sandra, you're letting the boys down. (*He smiles at her.*) Didn't they tell you? It's a team game.

SANDRA: No. No one mentioned it. (*She carries on working,*

33

consulting a file.) You know how vicars on trains are meant to carry *Playboy*. Only they have to cover it, so people don't see, with a copy of Proust. But coppers put Proust inside their *Playboy*.

BARRY: Proust? Is that that Swedish furniture store on the North Circular?

SANDRA: Oh sure, yeah. I expect you've bloody read it.

BARRY: He eats a biscuit, is that right?

SANDRA: You know perfectly well. You think it's clever to pretend to be stupid.

(*He looks at her a moment. Her back is turned to him.*)

BARRY: In this job, sometimes it is.

(*She catches his tone and turns from across the great distance directly to him.*)

SANDRA: Why didn't you say? If you already knew them? Why didn't you mention it?

BARRY: I didn't want anyone to know. It's clearer that way. It's simpler. I like a clear pond. Not muddy.

(SANDRA's *gaze doesn't waver*.)

SANDRA: So you lied?

BARRY: What? (*He leans forward, his ear cupped*.) What was that word? Do we have a dictionary? I'll just look it up.

(*She smiles*.)

SANDRA: And them?

BARRY: What?

SANDRA: No, it's something else that puzzles me. I mean, OK, I can see you decided to pretend not to recognize them. You've explained it. I sort of understand.

BARRY: Well?

(BARRY *stands, frowning slightly, waiting for her to go on*.)

SANDRA: That bit's easy. But the problem is, Barry . . . You see what I'm asking . . . Why did they pretend not to know you?

(*She frowns. There is a sudden silence. The atmosphere has changed. Before he can answer,* LESTER *comes hurrying back to go to a cupboard to look for something*.)

34

LESTER: Jeez Louise, it's one of those mornings. Esther can't find any gloves.

SANDRA: Gloves?

LESTER: For the body search.

(BARRY *has not moved. He is standing quite still in the middle of the room, as* DAVE *now returns.*)

Hello, Dave. They just had a call. It's a sudden death.

(*He turns at the cupboard and hands a quickly scrawled note to* DAVE. *As he does he frowns at* BARRY *and* SANDRA.)

What are you two doing? Sandra, wasting your time?

SANDRA: Yes, Sarge, you got it.

(*She moves to pull her coat and hat on.* DAVE *is very slowly putting on his gloves.*)

What about Dave? Shouldn't he be hurrying?

DAVE: Hardly. If it's a sudden death, it doesn't make any difference when I turn up.

(JIMMY *comes back from the cells impatiently.*)

JIMMY: Where are you, Barry? You on strike or something?

BARRY: Yeah, of course. I'm just on my way.

LESTER: He's still dreaming of the barmaid.

BARRY: Oh yeah, naturally.

LESTER: Are you going to tell us what she's actually like?

(*He has collected the gloves and is now doing some quick form-hunting.* DAVE *and* SANDRA *are both dressing to go out.* JIMMY *has moved to a filing cabinet to check records.*)

BARRY: Oh, extraordinary. She's really something. Don't you think so, Sandra?

SANDRA: How would I know?

BARRY: When aroused, she can spin the dial on a telephone with her nipples.

(LESTER *at once carries the Standing Orders book to another filing cabinet to look for another form.*)

LESTER: Thank you. That gives me an image to take through the day.

(BARRY *makes to go, but before he can,* TOBY *comes back from the cells.*)

TOBY: (*Urgently*) There's a pub fight, Sarge. Two scrotes in the Windmill tearing each other apart. (*He turns to* JIMMY.) And your body's throwing his chair round the room.

JIMMY: Oh shit.

(JIMMY *dashes off to collect the keys and runs off down the corridor. Meanwhile, from the other door, uniformed police are coming in, ready-dressed, to go to the pub fight.* JIMMY *nearly bumps into* ESTHER BALLY, *coming from the cells.*)

BARRY: Go for it, Jimmy.

ESTHER: Is anyone coming? I've got two naked women weeping and no bloody gloves.

(DAVE *turns at the main door, Rambo-like. The stage is suddenly full of blue serge.*)

DAVE: We're all going out.

LESTER: Yeah.

DAVE: Fighting crime.

(*There is just a second's suspension.* SANDRA *smiles.*)

SANDRA: Let's get them before they get us.

SCENE SIX

As the police turn to disperse their separate ways, the stage expands and BECKETT *leads* IRINA *through the wire-fenced courtyard that leads to the huge wing of the gaol. They are two small figures walking gingerly through the vast area.* IRINA *is smartly dressed, in coat and good shoes.*

BECKETT: All right, it's this way. (*As they approach, he points to the ground.*) Watch the shit packages.

IRINA: Oh yes. Goodness.

BECKETT: The prisoners throw them out of their windows.

IRINA: Yes. Yes, I see.

(*He lets her into the main well of the prison block. At once the stage darkens, with the high criss-cross light cutting through the Victorian gloom.*)

36

Thank you.

(*There is a single, scrubby table and two metal chairs with canvas seats.*)

What, it's some sort of protest?

BECKETT: No. It's not a protest. No, it's more they don't like the smell. (*He moves round the room arranging the table and chairs for her.*)

Have you been here before?

IRINA: No. Not to this one.

BECKETT: We get a lot of visitors . . .

IRINA: I'm sure.

BECKETT: Coming to look over this place. We have a name for them.

IRINA: Oh yes. What's that?

BECKETT: We call them Something-Must-Be-Dones. Oh look, we say, there's another bunch of Something-Must-Be-Dones. (*He looks around.*) This place is their monument.

IRINA: And is nothing done?

(*He looks at her a moment, a sudden quiet flash of real feeling.*)

BECKETT: Only by us, Miss Platt. It's left to us.

IRINA: Yes.

(*He looks her straight in the eye.*)

BECKETT: Still, I think the prisoners like it. Or why else do they keep coming back?

(GERARD *has appeared. The three of them stand a moment, silent in the vast area.* GERARD *is a little ghostly, more suited to his clothes now, which he has found a way of tucking in, but grey and still.*)

McKinnon?

GERARD: Yes?

BECKETT: This lady's come to see you. It's all yours. You can have as long as you like.

(BECKETT *turns and goes.* GERARD *does not move.* IRINA *hovers nervously by the table.*)

IRINA: This is kind. It's good of you to see me.

37

(*There is no reply.*)

Your solicitor is meant to be here but he hasn't turned up.

GERARD: No. (*He is watching her all the time.*) But then it's not very likely.

IRINA: Why's that?

GERARD: I don't know him very well.

(*There's a pause.*)

When he took me on as a client, he actually handed me a pen. It said, 'Trust me, I'm a solicitor.'

(IRINA *smiles, relieved he's talking.*)

I haven't seen hide nor hair of him since.

IRINA: No. I heard that.

GERARD: There was pen I'd seen which I wanted to give him in return. I saw it once in a shop at the seaside. It said, 'Don't jerk me off, I've already come.'

(*She looks at him a moment, assessing him.*)

IRINA: How is it here? How are you finding it?

GERARD: I tried to take a course, you know. There's a bookbinding course. I thought, that's interesting work. It takes four weeks. You learn how to do it. But then you can't practise until you get out. (*He looks at her unforgivingly.*) I thought, yeah, that's it: they give you something, then they take it away.

(*She is cool, appraising.*)

IRINA: I see. So that's how you're feeling . . .

GERARD: It is.

IRINA: You've already taken the role of 'Poor Me' . . .

(*There is a moment's pause while he assimilates this.*)

GERARD: Are you saying I shouldn't?

IRINA: No. You can do what you want to. (*She looks at him, unyielding now.*) But if you ask my opinion, it's the wrong way to go.

(*He looks at her a moment.*)

GERARD: I'm banged up with two other people. I shan't even tell you what they're doing all day. I have to watch them. And that warder tells me I'm not meant to get angry.

38

IRINA: Yes. (*She waits a moment.*) Well, I think he may have a point.

GERARD: Oh, may he?

IRINA: That's right. It's a question of self-preservation. It's none of my business, of course. But you can either moulder here in pointless self-pity. Or else you decide that you're going to fight.

(*He looks at her, mistrustfully.*)

GERARD: Fight how?

IRINA: I'd have thought it was obvious. Isn't it?

GERARD: It depends what you mean.

IRINA: I think you know. But I'm not quite sure why're being so coy about it.

(*He is standing, shifty now.*)

Your sentence was harsh. By any standards, it was ridiculous.

(*There is a moment's pause.*)

Why haven't you asked us for an appeal?

(*He looks at her a moment, then moves away. She moves towards the table, confident.*)

You see, the point is, I have been considering, ever since the trial, I've been thinking, you see. Our client was outside. He was the driver. There's been an obvious injustice. Each day I've been expecting his solicitor to get in touch with us. And it's worried me that we've heard nothing.

GERARD: You've been worried?

IRINA: Yes.

GERARD: You've thought of me?

(IRINA *smiles, getting his drift.*)

IRINA: Yes, I've been worried, and yes, I'm a lawyer. The two things can go together, you know.

(GERARD *smiles, warming to her.*)

GERARD: All right . . .

IRINA: I do know. Believe me, I do understand you. Our job is to process. We hand people on. That's what we do. And

39

like all other people, in all other parts of this system, we tend to forget you when you pass out of our view. But I suppose something, sometimes, rankles us. For no real reason perhaps. Something puzzles us.

GERARD: I puzzled you?

IRINA: Yes. If you like. Or . . . I don't know . . . you just like someone. You take a liking to them.
(*There is a pause.*)
And you decide that you'd like to help.
(GERARD *stands on the other side of the room, uncertain.*)

GERARD: It's hard.

IRINA: Yes.

GERARD: It isn't easy. (*He looks across at her in anguish.*) There are other people involved.

IRINA: Uh-huh.

GERARD: And I'm on my own.

IRINA: I can see. And you're frightened.
(*She waits a moment. He doesn't answer.*)
I'm on my own also. In my own way.
(*He looks at her, curious now.*)

GERARD: What does that mean?

IRINA: Oh just . . . my life's a bit tricky. I'm here independently. Sir Peter Edgecombe led your defence. As you haven't contacted us, he's been saying it isn't our business. He's actually quite hostile. He's saying we shouldn't waste our time. There are far more important things. The world is full of young criminals.
(GERARD *smiles slightly.*)

GERARD: So what did he say when you told him you wanted to come here today?
(IRINA *shifts.*)

IRINA: Well . . .

GERARD: No, really, I'm asking.

IRINA: I'm not sure it's relevant. I shouldn't have started this. We're not here to talk about me . . .

GERARD: No . . .

40

IRINA: And my problems . . .

GERARD: I know. But I kind of like it. To be honest, I'm finding it quite a relief.

(*He moves away, tense now.*)

GERARD: You have no idea. You go over and over. You think about nothing except your own case. It's your whole world. You go on re-living it. Till you think you'll go crazy.

IRINA: Yes. *So?*

(*She waits a moment.*)

That's what I'm saying. I know it's dangerous. But now you have to take the next step.

(GERARD *looks at her, grave.*)

The first thing is . . . did you do it?

(GERARD *just nods, not answering.*)

And your alibi?

GERARD: Nonsense.

IRINA: Well that's the first problem we have. You lied.

GERARD: I know.

IRINA: Well you'll be changing your story. (*She is suddenly direct, quiet.*) Why did you lie?

GERARD: 'Cos I'm scared. Scared, so I have to go to the lavatory. That sort of scared, do you know?

(*She smiles.*)

IRINA: Yes.

GERARD: Have you known that?

IRINA: Just . . . no, it's silly . . . (*She stops, embarrassed.*)

GERARD: Tell me.

IRINA: Once. When I was in love.

GERARD: Oh, really?

IRINA: Sure. When I thought of him. When I thought, oh, I'll see him today. Or tonight. Or I thought, I may lose him. My stomach turned over. (*She is taken aback by this sudden intimacy between them.*) I know it's not the same thing.

(GERARD *is now looking at her intently.*)

GERARD: Are you in love now?

IRINA: This was in Antigua.

GERARD: Is that where you're from?

(*She nods.*)

So are British men a let-down in comparison?

IRINA: I think we're straying right off the path.

GERARD: I know, but it's great.

(*He smiles, still looking at her, making her answer.*)

IRINA: To answer you . . . No. It's more . . . It's just difficult now, having known the real thing. Anything less, so to speak, seems sort of pointless. (*She smiles.*) People always tell me I'm unrealistic. Not just about love. In everyting. They say, 'All or nothing's no way to live.' But so many people seem to settle for so little.

GERARD: Maybe. Maybe most people don't have a choice.

(*There is a darkness in his tone which she catches, then looks down.*)

IRINA: Yes.

(GERARD *looks at her, as if making a silent pact. Then he starts slowly, as if finally released to tell his story.*)

GERARD: I came over, you know, I got the boat to Holyhead only two years ago. I hitch-hiked down the M1. That very first day, I was on that corner in Cricklewood. You know that corner?

IRINA: I do.

GERARD: You get a day's labouring, if you get there early. The vans come by, they pick you up about six.

IRINA: What happened to that?

GERARD: It was all the big houses, being refurbished. I saw some great houses. Then there was the slump.

IRINA: Yes.

GERARD: And I'd met a girl. (*He stops a moment.*)

IRINA: Well, that's great.

GERARD: Yes, it is. Then she was pregnant, so I got a job as a hospital porter. But we could only get a room above a pub. The noise was just dreadful. And the first child . . . (*He hesitates.*) Perhaps you've heard this . . . well, the child wasn't right.

IRINA: No.

42

(*She is still attentive, as if moving might break the spell.*)

GERARD: The pub is a little bit Republican, so there's a lot of singing. It can go on till four. So I started driving. We needed the money.

IRINA: At nights?

GERARD: Yes. To get stuff to the market.

IRINA: When did you sleep?

GERARD: When I got to the hospital. I'd kip in the laundry room. There were nurses who liked me.

IRINA: I can see why they should.

(*But* GERARD *is too absorbed now to notice what she says.*)

GERARD: I was thinking, you know, it's like the water's up to here . . . (*He draws a line across his neck.*) One big wave and I'm gone. Every week I just about survive and no more. Then Barbara was pregnant again. I was asked to do this job, I thought, OK, just the once. What everyone needs is one lump of money. And the waves will only be up to my chest.

(*He stands a moment, thinking.*)

IRINA: How much were you to get?

GERARD: Oh, not 'all or nothing' . . .

IRINA: No . . .

(*She smiles, acknowledging the reference.*)

GERARD: They don't give you the moon. Eight hundred. It's tempting. (*He thinks again a moment.*) It's pretty hard to say no.

(IRINA *takes out her notebook and lays it on the desk, not yet writing.*)

I'd run into Travis and Fielding. I'd met then first in a pub. Then they got in touch. The whole thing was terribly simple. The two of them went in, and I sat outside in the van, shit-scared, I admit. Then they came running out. They didn't even mention the bloke they'd tied up. (*He shrugs.*) I went home, you understand. I thought, that was easy. But I hadn't been paid. This was three days after the job. I went round to Fielding's place. It was bad luck. (*He hesitates a moment.*) We were just talking and in came the

43

detectives. They had a warrant. They were going to search that flat.

IRINA: Did they?

GERARD: Oh sure. They went into the bathroom. Then after a moment there, then they came out. (*He stops.*) They had a bag.

IRINA: A bag?

GERARD: Yes. They said they'd found this bag. He asked them to look in it.

IRINA: And they did?

GERARD: Yes.

IRINA: And how did Travis and Fielding react?

GERARD: (*Shrugs slightly*) They weren't surprised.

IRINA: Are you sure?

GERARD: It didn't surprise them. Fielding said, 'Oh, I thought you might find something like that.'

(IRINA *has begun to write now.*)

Then they looked at me. The detective said he thought I should go home.

(IRINA *thinks a moment.*)

IRINA: So did you then get in touch with Travis and Fielding?

GERARD: Well, sure, of course, I was going crazy. I called them, I said, look, I saw in that bag. They said, you didn't. You didn't see anything. If you saw anything, then that's the end. (*He looks at her a moment.*) Then they said, 'Look, when we're arrested, we've decided we're pleading not guilty. You need an alibi.' I said, 'No, I don't want to do that. Thinking up stories, perjuring witnesses.' They said, 'We're telling you.'

IRINA: They threatened you?

GERARD: They said in the past they'd used guns.

IRINA: Did you believe them?

GERARD: They mentioned Barbara. (*He looks at her a moment.*) Yeah, well there we are. Now do you see why I've not been in touch?

(IRINA *looks at him.*)

44

IRINA: And the bag . . .

GERARD: Yes?

IRINA: What was in it?

GERARD: Semtex. They said he planted it.

IRINA: Semtex?

GERARD: The copper planted it.

IRINA: Why? Gerard, why did he do that? Did they tell you?
(*He has turned away, not seeming to hear her for a moment.*)
I'm listening. Honestly. Gerard, I believe what you say.
But it's no good . . . the story's no good unless you give me a
reason.

GERARD: I'm afraid I have no idea.
(*There is barely a moment, and then a bell rings. They both
start. As they have been talking, evening has arrived. They are
both left with only high, grey light above them.*)

IRINA: What's that?

GERARD: It's tea. It's tea and recreation.
(IRINA *looks round, suddenly conscious of their isolation.*)

IRINA: My God, it's dark, they've forgotten us.
(*She looks at him – two people embarrassed at finding
themselves alone.*)
I must go. We should find someone. (*She gets up.*) May I
come back? May I come back tomorrow?

GERARD: Yes. Yes, I'd like that.

IRINA: Good. So would I. (*She looks at him a moment.*) I
shouldn't say this. It's irresponsible. They teach you at
college you must never do this. But you do have a friend
now. I promise you.
(GERARD *doesn't move.*)
Keep faith and I will. (*She looks down.*) I'll be in touch.

SCENE SEVEN

IRINA *goes, very quietly, leaving* GERARD *sitting alone, staring.
The lights on the stage change in silence, isolating* GERARD, *then at*

45

the other side of the stage finding BARRY *in exactly the same position, also staring out, his work desk untidy and overflowing in front of him, a night light burning on his desk, the empty police station behind him.*

The two men stare identically outwards, as in a dream. Then, very distantly, the first chords of the overture of Die Zauberflöte, *just heard, and* JIMMY, *silent, sharp-suited, steps like a ghost in immediately behind* BARRY. BARRY *doesn't turn.*

BARRY: Oh, it's you, Jimmy.
    (*He lifts a letter from the top of the desk and, without turning, hands it to* JIMMY, *who reads it.*)
JIMMY: So it's come.
BARRY: Yes.
JIMMY: You were expecting it.
BARRY: Not this soon.
JIMMY: They had to do it. Congratulations.
BARRY: I'm not sure I want it. I'm not sure I want to go without you.
    (JIMMY *frowns, disbelieving.*)
JIMMY: Oh, come on now, Barry . . .
BARRY: Policing's all to do with your partner.
JIMMY: You've got to go.
BARRY: Have I?
JIMMY: The Flying Squad? Sure.
    (*He steps forward,* BARRY *still not turning,* JIMMY *confident.*)
They owe you, Barry. You'll go. You're all policeman. You're the real thing.
    (*At the other side of the stage,* BECKETT *has stepped in beside* GERARD, *equally ghost-like, equally unobserved.* JIMMY *and* BARRY *hold where they are. The overture continues, eerily, in the background.*)
BECKETT: You all right, McKinnon?
GERARD: Yes, I'm fine, thank you.
BECKETT: You've missed your tea.
    (GERARD *turns, still in his dream.*)

We've lost you, I can tell. I know when it happens. For the next three months you're gone.

GERARD: Gone?

BECKETT: You'll be in Dreamland. They all go to Dreamland. You've got that vacant look on your face. For a while. They all get it. (*He smiles directly at* GERARD.) Did someone say something about an appeal?

(*Before he can answer,* BARRY, *sitting back in his chair, smiles and starts talking. The Mozart continues.*)

BARRY: It's funny, you know, just lately, sitting in traffic, I find myself thinking, how long have I got? How long before it wears me right down? I have a fantasy, I'll walk right out of it . . . (*He smiles.*) Or shall I wait till they kick me out?

(*At once, again, before* JIMMY *can answer,* BECKETT *moves in towards* GERARD, *shaking his head, the music building a little now.*)

BECKETT: Look, did that lawyer tell you it was terrible? Did she say a terrible injustice had been done? (*He gestures round the place.*) And how awful this prison is? (*He smiles.*) Then what did she do? I'll tell you. She walked away. Walk in. Upset them. Leave them. That's lawyers.

(GERARD *stands up and moves to the door, very quiet and calm.*)

GERARD: I believe in her. I think she's all right.

(*And as he says this, the Mozart suddenly catches fire, the violins kicking into the* allegro, *and the whole stage expands as* SIR PETER *and* IRINA, *the two of them in evening dress, walk up the main staircase towards the Crush Bar at the Royal Opera House.*)

SIR PETER: So you changed your mind about opera? Woody didn't seem to think it would interest you at all.

IRINA: Where did he get that idea? Goodness. How dare he?

SIR PETER: I was shocked. I thought I must be losing touch. I thought all educated young women loved music.

(IRINA *smiles.*)

IRINA: Yes, well, at the right moment, we do. (*They stop at the top of the stairs. She turns her back to him.*) Take my coat off.

SIR PETER: I'm sorry?

IRINA: Take my coat off.

(SIR PETER *hesitates a second, then he takes the coat from her back. Underneath she is bare-armed in a full-length evening dress. For a moment neither of them says anything.*)
All right?

SIR PETER: Yes. (*He hesitates, for once wrong-footed.*) Yes, fine.

IRINA: I wanted to ask you, I needed a word about Gerard McKinnon.

SIR PETER: McKinnon? Did you? Well, if you wish.

(*At this point,* GERARD *returns to his cell. He sits down on the edge of his bed, a thoughtful expression on his face. The stage is now divided into three: the opera house, the police station and the cell.* SIR PETER *smiles and leans in towards* IRINA, *pointing to some of the crowd in the Crush Bar.*)
Do you know Sir Hamish Tyrone over there?

IRINA: No.

SIR PETER: He's the Cabinet Secretary. That's the Lord Chief. You know him, of course.

IRINA: Tell me, if you run the country, is it compulsory to go to the opera in the evening?

(SIR PETER *smiles, enjoying himself.*)

SIR PETER: You tell me. I have no idea.

(GERARD *turns a moment, as if hearing something. In the other part of the stage,* JIMMY *stirs, trying to reach* BARRY, *who is staring gloomily into space.*)

JIMMY: You're always saying it's impossible. You say it's all a lost art. But we did it last week.

BARRY: Just. By the skin of our teeth.

(SIR PETER *and* IRINA, *carrying their programmes, move on down towards us.*)

IRINA: Well, what's your answer?

(SIR PETER *thinks a moment, serious.*)

SIR PETER: You know as well as I do, the young man did everything wrong. He told a complete pack of lies. He

48

persisted in them long after he should. I don't have to tell you the Appeal Court will be starkly prejudiced against him. (*He pauses. Then he's quiet.*) But if you want me to, I'll take it on.

(*They stand a moment.* IRINA *smiles. They arrive at the auditorium and opposite them now are the huge red curtains of the Royal Opera House. Meanwhile, the other areas come to life.* BECKETT *and two other screws patrol down the corridor outside the cells.*)

BARRY: Shall we get a drink?

SIR PETER: Is there time for a drink?

BECKETT: Lights out! Lights out!

(*The lights start to go out in the prison.*)

BARRY: Let's have a frame of snooker.

JIMMY: Great.

(*As they start to move off,* BARRY *smiles easily at* JIMMY.)

BARRY: Oh, by the way, will you keep quiet about the Flying Squad?

JIMMY: Surely.

BARRY: Just for now. Keep it to yourself.

(*They both grin.* BARRY *is standing directly opposite* JIMMY *and now he puts his hands on his shoulders.*)

A man's got to have some secrets. Hasn't he?

(*The two men embrace.* SIR PETER *and* IRINA *take their seats.*)

JIMMY: Aren't you meant to call Sandra?

BARRY: Sandra? Who's Sandra?

(*The two men head off, arm in arm.* IRINA *turns to* SIR PETER, *as the curtain rises.*)

IRINA: The opera's starting. I'm ready for this.

WARDERS: Lights out! Lights out!

(*The curtain rises. The opening chords of the first act ring out.*)

49

ACT TWO

SCENE ONE

As the audience return, we find that guests are gathering in a panelled ante-room in Lincoln's Inn. They are all dressed in white tie and tails, for a formal dinner in the Hall. The High Table is visible beyond, in the Hall itself, laid out magnificently, with each place marked by four different wine glasses. The Inn's best silver is on display. Candles burn.

The TOASTMASTER *is calling out the names of the arrivals, one by one.*

TOASTMASTER: Mr Sylvester Pike QC.
His Grace the Bishop of Bath and Wells.
His Excellency Al Hadji Sulay Ibrahim Dunko.
Mr Jonathan Farrell.
The Right Honourable the Earl of Evesham.
Mr Derek Carver.
(*At the side of the stage is Gerard's prison cell, the warders patrolling in the far distance. And as the lights go down in the auditorium,* GERARD *looks up to a grey square of light above him at the cell window, as the main scene in Lincoln's Inn freezes.*)

GERARD: Six o'clock is the worst. That's when it hits you. When you sense the evening outside. Listening to the traffic. You were served your supper at four thirty. And now you're being told it's the end of the day. (*He pauses a moment.*) Calm down, Gerard. Don't get excited. Each day I watch the evening come down. Just the grey, stretched like a tent over London. And the rain. And the smell of the kitchens, waiting for tomorrow. (*He is still.*) Oh God, let me not give in to hope.

50

At once, as if in response to GERARD, *the main scene animates itself as lawyers and barristers murmur in anticipation. Here, a massively distinguished group has already formed.* CUDDEFORD, *wearing tails, is moving across to welcome a tall, apparently genial man in his fifties who is just arriving.*

TOASTMASTER: The Home Secretary. The Right Honourable Charles Kendrick MP.
(*Before he has a moment, the* HOME SECRETARY *finds* CUDDEFORD *beside him.*)

CUDDEFORD: Home Secretary, welcome. We are honoured to have you here.

HOME SECRETARY: Thank you.

CUDDEFORD: For one of our Grand Days. You are Guest of Honour, of course.

HOME SECRETARY: You don't need to say that. In such distinguished company. What do I see? An ex-prime minister, an earl and a high commissioner?
(*He looks round the group where an African politician in tribal robes is notably resplendent. A number of the men are wearing medals.*)

CUDDEFORD: Yes. We've been trawling.

HOME SECRETARY: Indeed.

TOASTMASTER: The Governor of the Bank of England.

CUDDEFORD: With a rather fine net. (*He smiles at the* HOME SECRETARY.) We knew the law was not in your background.

HOME SECRETARY: No. No, I was an accountant.

CUDDEFORD: Yes, well, that's right. So we thought you might like to drink in the atmosphere, so that you were more fully informed.

HOME SECRETARY: Well, thank you.

CUDDEFORD: So you'd have some real, human faces in your mind when it came to making vital decisions.

HOME SECRETARY: Yes.

(*The* WAITER *comes with a tray of glasses.*)

CUDDEFORD: Champagne?

HOME SECRETARY: Thank you

CUDDEFORD: Please. Leave the fishy stuff there.

(*The* HOME SECRETARY *takes a glass of champagne. The* WAITER *puts a pot of caviare down next to them on a small table.*)

HOME SECRETARY: Yes, it's good to have a context for any important policy debate.

CUDDEFORD: Yes, that's right. (*He smiles.*) Believe me, the judges understand, in all questions dealing with the future of the Bar, the government must act. It must do whatever it thinks best. But always within the framework of the constitution.

HOME SECRETARY: Yes. (*He looks at* CUDDEFORD *a moment, wary.*) Well, surely.

CUDDEFORD: But you hardly need me to remind you of that.

HOME SECRETARY: No.

(*The* TOASTMASTER *has already begun to announce the next arrival.*)

TOASTMASTER: Sir Peter Edgecombe QC.

(*They turn at once to greet* SIR PETER, *immaculate in white tie.*)

HOME SECRETARY: Good Lord, look who's here.

CUDDEFORD: Do you know Sir Peter?

HOME SECRETARY: Do I know Sir Peter?

(*He repeats the question as if it were ridiculous. They shake hands warmly.*)

SIR PETER: Welcome, Charles. So, how are you?

HOME SECRETARY: I was talking only yesterday to the Prime Minister. You'll be pleased to hear that your name came up.

SIR PETER: Oh, really? (*He smiles involuntarily.*) How interesting.

CUDDEFORD: That's good for you, Peter.

SIR PETER: Yes.

HOME SECRETARY: We actually discussed you for quite a long time.

SIR PETER: I'm very flattered.

HOME SECRETARY: We couldn't work it out. We were both wondering why on earth you took the Piaf.

(CUDDEFORD *smiles, delighted.* SIR PETER *looks miffed.*)

CUDDEFORD: Yes, that question has puzzled some of us here.

SIR PETER: I don't think it should monopolize our conversation. When there are so many more important issues in the air.

HOME SECRETARY: Goodness. Are there? (*He says this mildly, smiling, then, in order to divert the conversation, picks up a menu card from the table.*) 'Roast Venison Baden-Baden'. Just exactly how is that done?

CUDDEFORD: (*Smiles*) I think you'll find it's a young roebuck.

HOME SECRETARY: Ah, yes.

CUDDEFORD: It's been shot through the heart and then skinned. Then basted in some sort of fruity, substantial gravy.

HOME SECRETARY: Good gracious.

CUDDEFORD: Then it's served up to us.

(*He smiles. The* HOME SECRETARY *watches him, a little bemused, but too old a hand to let himself show it.*)

As you know, we have a system whereby law students have to eat dinners to qualify.

HOME SECRETARY: I've heard that.

CUDDEFORD: They have to eat their way through twenty-four dinners in all. We were proposing to abolish this requirement as outdated. But then we found that without this, so to speak, ready-made pool of captive consumers, the entire kitchen effort would not be economic.

HOME SECRETARY: That's tricky.

CUDDEFORD: Hence we would not be able to give ourselves luncheon.

(*The* HOME SECRETARY *looks at* SIR PETER.)

53

SIR PETER: It's true.

CUDDEFORD: And that, of course, would be catastrophic.

HOME SECRETARY: I see that.

CUDDEFORD: The law is a college. We meet. We talk. A judge perhaps has a word with a barrister. He says nothing overt. Nothing critical. Maybe only a look, a chance remark. And yet all the time . . . there are hints. Thanks to these a barrister is learning. The social *is* the professional. (*He smiles*.) How do you put a true price on that?

HOME SECRETARY: Well, it's hard . . .

CUDDEFORD: It's not quantifiable.

HOME SECRETARY: No.

(CUDDEFORD *looks him in the eye*.)

CUDDEFORD: It adds to a richness of culture, a depth, a breadth of vision you only find in an Inn.

(*The* HOME SECRETARY *again looks across to* SIR PETER.)

SIR PETER: He's right.

CUDDEFORD: For instance, tonight, when the loyal toast is proposed, we do not rise. Did you know this?

HOME SECRETARY: Why, no.

CUDDEFORD: By special dispensation. From Charles the Second, no less. At a dinner here, he gave permission, in perpetuity, that this would be the only place in the kingdom where people do not rise to say God Save the King.

HOME SECRETARY: I'm astonished.

CUDDEFORD: He did it because he himself was too drunk to stand up. (*He nods, suddenly incisive*.) Now it's *this*, it's this sort of thing, Home Secretary . . .

HOME SECRETARY: Charles, please . . .

CUDDEFORD: What would you call it? This slow *silting* of tradition, this centuries-long building-up, this accumulation of strata, which makes the great rock on which we now do things. It's infinitely precious.

HOME SECRETARY: (*Frowns*) Yes, but it must also be open to change.

CUDDEFORD: (*Enthusiastically*) *Open*.

HOME SECRETARY: It must not become hidebound.

CUDDEFORD: Hidebound?

HOME SECRETARY: Yes.

CUDDEFORD: Small chance of that! (*He leans forward, sure of himself.*) Remember, all the time judging brings you in touch with ordinary people. In our courts. We see them every day. Ordinary, common-as-muck individuals. Some of them quite ghastly, I promise you that. (*He nods.*) This makes us alert to public opinion. We're closer to it, perhaps, than you think.

HOME SECRETARY: Are you?

CUDDEFORD: It's reflected in the way we sentence. Everyone claims it's our fault if we sentence too high. But the tariff for rape . . .

HOME SECRETARY: I know . . .

CUDDEFORD: . . . has shot up from what?

HOME SECRETARY: I know this . . .

CUDDEFORD: Maybe eighteen months deferred to over five years. It's not at *our* wish. It's because we have listened to what the public, at least the female part of it, wants us to do.

(*The* HOME SECRETARY *is smiling, familiar with this argument.*)

HOME SECRETARY: Yes, I admit. But it's a rare exception. There are figures from Germany. Did you read those?

CUDDEFORD: (*Frowns*) Germany? No.

HOME SECRETARY: I sent them over. I circulated all High Court judges.

CUDDEFORD: I read little from Germany.

(*He turns to* SIR PETER, *diverting, but the* HOME SECRETARY *is not letting him off the hook.*)

Like most judges, I have no time to read, off the case. Maybe if I'm lucky, a thriller . . .

HOME SECRETARY: There they've reduced all prison sentences radically, by up to one-quarter, even one-third, without

55

any effect on the criminal statistics.

(CUDDEFORD *looks at him warily.*)

CUDDEFORD: Really? Germany?

HOME SECRETARY: The same is true in Sweden.

CUDDEFORD: Sweden? (*He turns to* SIR PETER.) Peter, had you heard this?

SIR PETER: No. No, actually. (*He looks down, feeling himself on thin ice.*) Word hadn't reached me.

CUDDEFORD: It hadn't reached me either. (*He frowns.*) I think it's to do with the mail.

(*The* HOME SECRETARY *looks at him a little more severely, finally showing a little steel.*)

HOME SECRETARY: Yes, it's a fact, it's true, government is nervous of bullying. As you pointed out, the constitutional proprieties must be observed.

CUDDEFORD: Indeed.

HOME SECRETARY: Yes, they must. But, to be frank, we're reaching a point where we'll run out of ways of requesting the judiciary to be less *trigger-happy*.

(CUDDEFORD *looks at him a moment, noting the last word.*) I know, of course, it's none of my business . . .

CUDDEFORD: Well . . .

HOME SECRETARY: I'm only the Home Secretary, I wouldn't dream of interfering . . .

CUDDEFORD: No.

HOME SECRETARY: I know how wrong that would be. Constitutionally.

CUDDEFORD: It would.

HOME SECRETARY: An independent judiciary is perhaps the most important bullwark against chaos this country has. (*He looks* CUDDEFORD *in the eye.*) But we've nowhere to put all these bloody prisoners you keep sending us. (*He checks himself, impeccably polite.*) And that is something you must take on board.

(CUDDEFORD *just looks at him.*)

CUDDEFORD: Yes.

56

HOME SECRETARY: Why can't you see that?

CUDDEFORD: We do. (*He moves towards him, smiling, quiet now.*) We do, Home Secretary. But truly it is your problem, not ours.

(*Before the* HOME SECRETARY *can respond, he goes on.*) You see, just think, if for one single moment, when I'm at work in my court, if I begin to consider . . . if I ever consider what prison is now like . . . then I cannot fairly administer justice. Because my head is full of what we may call failings of society . . . (*He shakes his head regretfully.*) Which are truly not my concern. (*He looks at the* HOME SECRETARY.) It's actually dangerous. If I and my colleagues begin to deceive ourselves, if we fudge our principles, if when the accused stands before us, some extraneous factor, however pressing, makes us pretend that crime is not crime, and should not be punished, then the judges become an instrument of government convenience. (*He smiles.*) And, as you said earlier, that is not what you want.

(*The* HOME SECRETARY *looks at him warily.*)

HOME SECRETARY: No.

CUDDEFORD: Believe me, I know, I do understand you. Tonight in your cells, I appreciate you have twice as many prisoners as places. It's sad. It's regrettable. These poor devils, they prey on my mind.

HOME SECRETARY: Then why don't you act?

(CUDDEFORD *looks at him and smiles, not taking the question seriously, but turning good-humouredly to* SIR PETER.)

CUDDEFORD: Haven't I explained? Haven't I just said to you? (*He leans in, taking the* HOME SECRETARY's *arm.*) And mightn't I ask the same thing of you?

(*Before he can say more, the* TOASTMASTER *interrupts.*)

TOASTMASTER: My Lords, Ladies and Gentlemen, dinner is served.

(CUDDEFORD *pats the* HOME SECRETARY's *arm*

57

good-humouredly, before heading off to find the HIGH
COMMISSIONER.)

CUDDEFORD: And now we've talked enough shop. Where's the
High Commissioner? Take your places, please, everyone,
before we go in.

(*The* HOME SECRETARY *puts his glass down as everyone
teams up with a partner and gets into an orderly line of twos,
preparatory to going in.* SIR PETER *hovers, waiting for the*
HOME SECRETARY.)

HOME SECRETARY: What do you say, Peter?

SIR PETER: I say there's one thing to be grateful for.

HOME SECRETARY: Oh yes. And what's that?

SIR PETER: The British police.

HOME SECRETARY: (*Frowns*) I'm not sure I know what you
mean.

SIR PETER: It is one of the great mercies of your situation that
only 3 per cent of all crimes reach the courts. (*He smiles.*)
Just imagine the scale of your problems if the police began
to have some significant success. *— saying police are
inefficient*

HOME SECRETARY: Yes, I must say.

SIR PETER: The system is already strained to breaking point
by a force which is catching scarcely anyone at all.
(*They find themselves the pair at the end of the line.* SIR
PETER *reaches for his arm to draw him in to the crocodile.*)
Charles, you do have that to be grateful for.
(CUDDEFORD *is standing next to the High Commissioner at
the head of the line.* SIR PETER *and the* HOME SECRETARY
are at the back.)

CUDDEFORD: Gentlemen, the bell is about to be rung.
(*The stage is suddenly still and the whole Hall falls quiet. A
bell sounds. The lights go out and the group stands a moment
in the darkness, the lights of the candles burning far from
them. They set off in an orderly crocodile and make their way
in silence to the table. When they get there, each goes to his
place.* CUDDEFORD *is standing at the centre.*)
The eyes of all things look up and put their trust in Thee,

58

O Lord. Thou Givest them their Meat in Due Season, Thou Openest Thine Hands and fillest with Thy blessing every living Thing. Replenish our Hearts with Joy and Gladness that We, having sufficient, may be Rich and Plentiful in good works. God Save Thy Church, the Queen, the Royal Family and this Realm; God Send us Peace and Truth in Christ Our Lord.

ALL: Amen.

SCENE THREE

At once, in contrast to the previous scene, sirens howl and blue lights flash as we go to the charge room at night. But inside the police station at night the image is suspended, coppers working on their papers in the dim electric light, like children sitting for exams. The boisterousness of the day has, for a moment, passed as JIMMY *moves forward to address us, some sheets of paper in his hand.*

JIMMY: Already, you know, you can see the ones you fancy. It gets to be obvious after a while. I can throw my eyes down a crime sheet, and pick the ones where I'll get a result. (*He holds up the list to show the audience.*) There's maybe thirty-five cases. Most of them you haven't got a chance. Like burglaries, muggings, forget it, unless someone caught them red-handed. Which, if they did, it sure wasn't us. An officer on the beat witnesses, actually witnesses, one crime every ten years. Then maybe the case you choose isn't moving very quickly. What happens? Some pen-pusher comes down from upstairs, says, look, the local press are on to us, we need a nice graph. And please bear in mind, it's kind of important, visually speaking, a clear-up graph is meant to go up. (*He relaxes, enjoying himself.*) So you go down the club, you pull in seven kids. You do them for possession, let them off with a caution, and everything's fine. Seven crimes, seven

59

clear-ups. Oh yes, they all count. And everyone's happy with cautions. None of that senseless ferrying, none of those expensive appearances in court. It's public relations. We know that. So does everyone. Except for the public, of course. But public relations is always a bit of a toupee. If you can tell what it is, then it's not any good.

(*At once a* YOUNG POLICEMAN *and* WPC *appear, struggling with two immigrants, one* MAN, *one* WOMAN. *The* MAN *is protesting at being held while the* WOMAN *is keeping up an unceasing line of complaint about her rights. As they come through the charge-room door, making a racket,* JIMMY *goes back to consult the charge-room book.*)

MAN: Choldo! Mey keyta hun mujhey choldo!

WOMAN: Tumara haq nahi hai. Tum yey nahi kurr suktey. Yey kanoon kay khelaf hai. Mujhey vakil sey millney kar haq hai.

MAN: Mujhey haat mutt legow.

LESTER: Toby! Toby!

YOUNG POLICEMAN: Come on, now, come on, stop pissing me about now! (*He suddenly loses his temper.*) Stop pissing me about!

(*And he begins to get pretty rough as he bundles the* MAN *towards the cells.*)

WOMAN: Humarey dost Heathrow pay hai, Humarey sarey jaaney walley Heathrow pay hai. Yey humara haq hai. Tumara koi haq nahi bunta yey kurr ney keyliey.

MAN: Choldo! Choldo!

(LESTER *now stands in the middle of the room and shouts at* TOBY *to get him to go and help.*)

LESTER: Go and sort them . . .

TOBY: All right, all right . . .

LESTER: Go and sort them. Give Micky a hand with that lot. I don't care what you do to them. I can't bloody stand it. I've bloody had it for today.

TOBY: I'm going, don't worry . . .

(*From the other direction comes* ESTHER *in her police shirt,*

60

with her skirt worn very tight, with black stockings, a pile of documents under her arm.)

ESTHER: Come on, now, Lester, don't lose your rag.

(JIMMY *appears, his work obviously disturbed, from the CID room. He is in his shirt-sleeves, but manages to look as elegant as usual.*)

JIMMY: What's up?

LESTER: Immigration cases. We're holding them for Hounslow. I've already rung Hounslow five times.

ESTHER: Of course you have, darling.

(JIMMY *just smiles at* ESTHER, *as* LESTER *gathers up the things he needs.*)

LESTER: I hate immigration. Domestics. Drunks.

(ESTHER *puts her papers down right next to him and bumps her hip into him in a comradely way.*)

And bloody women.

ESTHER: Yeah, I've heard you hate us as well.

(*The noise from the cells is beginning to stop. The shouting has finished but the banging goes on.*)

JIMMY: It's his mother's fault.

ESTHER: You're kidding. What did she do to you?

LESTER: She didn't do anything. She just told me one day you all had an extra pair of teeth. (*He smiles at her quickly, looking up from the desk.*) I'm not saying where.

JIMMY: What he means is, he's never found them.

LESTER: No, but I've had fun looking.

JIMMY: Esther'll show you hers if you like.

(LESTER *is now on his way out, at speed.* ESTHER *flashes a smile at* JIMMY.)

ESTHER: Yeah. They're perfect. I've had fabulous bridgework.

(LESTER *jumps a little way into the air and shudders.*)

LESTER: Oh, my God, I can't wait.

(*As he goes out he passes* DAVE LAWRENCE, *who is coming back from the direction of the cells with a black man in his thirties, very large but very gentle, wearing khaki trousers and an American jacket. His name is* JASON SMITH, *and he is*

61

very distressed. DAVE *is carrying a print-out which he takes straight to the duty desk.* JIMMY *has wandered round and is now standing checking the night's crime list.*)

JASON: Don't do this to me, I beg of you. Look, I beg of you, I was just at a party, all right?

JIMMY: OK, Dave?

DAVE: Yes, fine.

(DAVE *gives a nod of recognition.* JASON *is carrying some photos, which he now holds up.*)

JASON: It's my mate. Look at this. All right? He's sitting on a tank. Tomorrow he's going to the desert. Imagine that. Be fair. Just imagine it.

(DAVE *has calmly taken out a form and is taking little notice.*)

DAVE: I think I can imagine it. Look, put away the happy snaps.

JASON: You don't know my wife. She'll kill me. I promise you, she'll kill me when she finds out.

(ESTHER *looks at him, a quick glance, then away as* JASON *persists.*)

Why me? Why did you choose me?

DAVE: We didn't choose you.

JASON: You did. There's thousands out there.

DAVE: You went through a red light.

JASON: It wasn't red. It was orange.

DAVE: Well, it doesn't matter.

JASON: So I lose my licence. Are you saying that's it?

DAVE: It's an automatic penalty. You're reading 70. For a 70 reading, it's automatic. (*He looks up a moment.*) I'm sorry, mate, there's nothing I can do.

(LESTER *comes back, still frazzled, walking heavily back to his place. The noise from the cells has stopped.* JIMMY *has taken over the crime book and gone to look it over in the corner.* ESTHER *is standing, writing on top of a filing cabinet.* JASON *moves now to the centre of the room to address everyone. They ignore him.*)

JASON: I don't get it. I don't bloody get it. I'm always there for

62

you. I'm a bloody builder. A builder, all right? Can't you tell the difference? (*He suddenly turns, furious.*) What's the point? What's the point of trying? Why bother to be normal? If you go through with this, I tell you what I'll do. I'm going to get a bobble hat and grow bloody dreadlocks. Because if this is what happens, I might as well.

(*There is silence in the room. Everyone carries on working.*) Why do you choose us? The law-abiding people? There's so much scum on the street. Why not pick up the scum? I'm always there for you, I see an accident, it's me that gets out, says, 'Can I help you, officer?' I help you. I always help. Why pick on me? I'm not a pusher. I'm not a pimp. (*He shakes his head.*) You want to know how to piss off law-abiding citizens?

DAVE: Thanks, but we feel we've got that licked already.

JASON: Do you know this saying? We've got a saying. Have you heard this? We call people 'rubber heels'.

DAVE: Yes.

JASON: We use it. We use it for people who creep up and bugger their own.

(*At this last remark of* JASON'*s,* LESTER *suddenly blows his top, throwing his chair back as he gets up, and honing in on* JASON *with real power.*)

LESTER: All right, that's enough of this, I've heard enough of this.

(*A couple of people look up at* LESTER'*s explosion, but nobody says anything.*)

At a 70 reading, you can actually kill people. You can kill with a car. If your blood level's at 70, you're a major liability. You can kill yourself at the same time.

(JASON *is looking at him, stunned.*)

All right, I shan't pretend that really matters. Why should it? You've acted like a prick.

JASON: I know.

(*He pauses, the wind suddenly gone out of him. The two big*

63

men are standing directly opposite each other in the middle of the room, and now JASON's *manner, in a drinker's switch, changes from angry to pathetic.*)

I know I have.

LESTER: But I'm only interested in protecting the public. Who may get killed by people like you.

(JASON *nods, contrite.*)

JASON: I want to say sorry.

LESTER: All right.

JASON: OK.

(LESTER *stands a moment, hands on hips, letting* JASON *calm down.*)

I'm going down on my knees.

(JASON *suddenly kneels in front of* LESTER *in the middle of the room. There is a sudden, uneasy silence throughout the room.*)

ESTHER: Anyone want tea?

JASON: I'm on my knees to you, skip. My wife and I, we're going through changes. Think. I'm a builder. I lose my licence, I tell you, I'm nothing. Without a licence, I'm nothing. I'm a Paddy in the Falls Road. I can't pay the bills, skip. I lose my licence, and what can I do?

(*There is a long silence.* LESTER *stands, uncomfortable.* JIMMY *doesn't look up.*)

JIMMY: I hate it when they grovel.

(DAVE *is quite still, just watching.*)

DAVE: You better get up, mate. I don't have that power. Nor does he. It's not up to us. It's a process, all right?

(SANDRA *comes in, in shirt-sleeves, and sees the kneeling man at* LESTER's *feet.*)

SANDRA: Hello, what's this? A proposal of marriage?

(LESTER *moves away, back to his seat.* DAVE *moves over to help* JASON *up.*)

DAVE: Come on, old mate.

SANDRA: Gosh, Lester, you're marrying a client. When's the happy day?

64

(LESTER *scowls at her.*)
Good evening, Jimmy.

JIMMY: Hello, Sandra.

(LESTER *frowns at the file she is carrying.*)

LESTER: What's that? CID file?

SANDRA: Oh yes, sure. No, it's nothing. I've just been looking. At something from an old job. An old case.

(*She moves a little quickly away from* LESTER *with the file, as* ESTHER *turns with a glossy document in her hand. She holds it up.*)

ESTHER: I'm meant to be organizing the divisional ski-ing party. Anyone fancy it?

SANDRA: No, thanks, Esther.

DAVE: In a moment, we're going to fingerprint you.

(SANDRA *goes to a desk at the side of the room where she sits to write out notes from her notebook.* JASON *is being led out, shaking his head, by* DAVE.)

JASON: I wouldn't do this to you.

DAVE: And then you're going to be charged formally. And then we'll put you in a taxi, all right?

(*They go.* ESTHER *is beside* LESTER *with the glossy brochure.*)

ESTHER: Fun on the slopes, yes, Lester?

LESTER: No, thank you, honestly. I don't think my marriage would last.

(JIMMY *chuckles.*)

JIMMY: Can he bring his wife? That's what Lester means.

LESTER: Don't even mention her. Do you know she's found a new word?

ESTHER: What's that?

LESTER: I think she sits reading dictionaries. I got in from the relief at seven thirty this morning, she was still in bed. I got in, she said, 'You know what our relationship needs?'

(ESTHER *smiles.*)

ESTHER: I can't think.

LESTER: 'What I'd like', she said, 'is less sex and more cherishing.' (*He shakes his head and looks round the room.*)

65

Cherishing! Does anyone know what that means? (*He smiles across at* JIMMY.) You do any cherishing, Jimmy?

JIMMY: Not consciously.

ESTHER: You can cherish on the slopes, if you like. That's what we go for. Well, at least, cherishing and drinking.

LESTER: Oh, well, in that case, I might come along.

(*They both smile.* ESTHER *moves away as* BARRY *comes in, in shirt-sleeves, carrying the usual polystyrene cup of coffee, a file, and various metal objects in evidence bags.*)

BARRY: Abstracting electricity! Is that the most boring crime of all time?

(JIMMY *looks up. But* SANDRA, *working at the back, doesn't turn.*)

JIMMY: Barry.

ESTHER: I don't know what it is.

LESTER: Fiddling the meter.

ESTHER: Oh, I see.

BARRY: In this case, at a squat! At a squat! For about fifteen quid. I mean, can you think of anything more pointless?

LESTER: What, than them doing it? Or us pursuing it?

BARRY: Both. Either. Who gives a damn? (*He tosses the evidence bags down on the desk and sits down, addressing the whole room.*) I mean, do you give a damn? (*He shakes his head.*) I read this statistic. If you take all the crime, all of it, every single bit, in money it doesn't add up to what's lost every year in tax evasion. (*He gestures round the huge room.*) And yet look at us! Here we all are.

LESTER: Sure.

BARRY: One hundred and thirty thousand policemen. Twenty-eight thousand in London alone.

YOUNG POLICEMAN: I'm going back out, Sarge.

BARRY: To collect a sum of money – at incredible expense – which is actually less than the government happily lets rich bastards get up and walk away with every year. (*He shakes his head. Everyone ignores him.*) I mean, please tell me, what is the point?

66

(LESTER *smiles and gets up*.)

LESTER: I can't answer that, Barry.

BARRY: Come on, I'm asking you.

LESTER: It's too deep for me. All right, Dave? (*On the way out he puts a friendly hand on* BARRY'*s shoulder*.) You should go on *Mastermind*. Come on, Esther, I'm going to do yours as well.

ESTHER: I'm coming. I'm on my way.

(ESTHER *follows* LESTER *out*. JIMMY *has got up and is sorting through the things* BARRY'*s thrown down*. SANDRA *has still not turned round*.)

JIMMY: You didn't see the Super?

BARRY: No, I didn't.

JIMMY: The boss is after us. Guess why.

(BARRY *smiles*.)

Too much overtime.

BARRY: Oh, you don't say.

JIMMY: He says we're way over budget. He says we've been coming on at five for surveillance without waking him up and asking him first.

(JIMMY *is gathering his stuff up now*.)

BARRY: So what's he going to do? Impound my BMW?

JIMMY: He says he knows exactly how you got that new set of steel wheels.

BARRY: Well, he's *right*. By catching thieves. That's how I got them. By getting up at five and doing the job.

(*He has a sort of generalized ill humour, but* JIMMY'*s heard it before*.)

JIMMY: Yeah, OK . . .

BARRY: But, of course, that's way out of fashion. We should all sit in the nick and make policy drafts. It's what we all say. It's all public relations.

JIMMY: Sure. It doesn't bother me. (*He looks up, smiling*.) Because *I'm* public relations. I'd have to be stupid not to know that. (*He laughs as he heads out of the room*.) When your name is Abdul, and they all call you Jimmy, it does

67

give you a certain perspective on things.

(*And* JIMMY's *gone.* BARRY *just smiles, agreeing with him, almost not noticing that he and* SANDRA *are now alone.*)

BARRY: Yeah, we're all part of it. Define your objectives. Fulfil your flow chart. Manage your resources. Keep your paper straight.

(*He turns, finding himself abandoned in the huge room.* SANDRA *is still facing away.*)

Hello. How are you?

SANDRA: Fine.

BARRY: I haven't seen you.

SANDRA: No.

(*And now for the first time she turns and looks at him. She is very quiet.*)

I wonder why not.

(BARRY *frowns.*)

I waited for you.

BARRY: Did you?

SANDRA: Yes. At the usual place.

BARRY: Oh, shit, really? I had a rugby match. I meant to say. (*He looks at her briefly, then away.*) Sometimes I do get tired of the secrecy. It makes the whole thing seem silly. Assignations. Times and places.

SANDRA: Yes. But perhaps you should have called me. Perhaps if you'd called me, I wouldn't have felt effed and left.

(BARRY *waits a moment, not wanting to rise to this.*)

BARRY: No.

SANDRA: Besides, I always thought you rather liked secrecy. I thought you got a buzz from it. Not looking at each other when we're at work. Having one over them. Don't you rather like that? Isn't having secrets your favourite thing? (*She waits.*) What's changed your mind?

BARRY: Nothing's changed.

SANDRA: Hasn't it?

BARRY: No. (*He waits a moment, uncomfortable.*) Why don't

68

we talk about it next week? When we're on day relief? It's easier. I think I'm too tired.

SANDRA: What, and you've got a headache as well?

(*He smiles, trying to keep it light.*)

BARRY: Come on, Sandra, this isn't like you.

SANDRA: I'm always so easy, is that what you mean?

BARRY: I didn't have you down as a nagger.

SANDRA: Thanks, Barry. But ask the boys, they'll tell you, all women are.

(*He turns to look at her, trying to apologize.*)

BARRY: I'm sorry. It's just a bad time. You try to keep cheerful. It's part of the job. (*He smiles.*) I used to think, at the end of my marriage, you know, in the last days with Kay, if you're a copper it's a bit pointless trying. You come home. 'Oh, can you wash my shirt, darling? It's got gob all over it. Yeah, I got spat on in the street. No, it didn't bother me. I'll just go upstairs and read to the kid.'

(*He looks down, thoughtful now.* SANDRA *just watches, not reacting.*)

All that stuff makes you cautious.

SANDRA: I know that.

BARRY: The job does.

SANDRA: I know.

(*There's a pause.*)

What are you saying? That I get too close?

BARRY: No. Not you. No. Never. (*He turns and looks at her.*) Never you, Sandra.

(*She waits a moment.*)

SANDRA: Then, what?

(*She waits for him to go on, but he says nothing more.*)

I think this is to do with McKinnon. And Travis. And Fielding.

BARRY: Do you?

SANDRA: Yes.

(*It is suddenly completely quiet in the station, the two of them tense now across the room.*)

69

Because something happened. I talked to you that day when we were in here. Then next day – wham – the iron curtain came down. (*She is very quiet.*) You forget. I know you, Barry. It's very insulting. I'm on your side. Don't you know that?
(*He is just looking at her thoughtfully, giving nothing away.*) What happened in the flat?

BARRY: Nothing. Nothing. Really. I promise you.

SANDRA: It's me. (*She waits.*) It's me, Barry.

BARRY: So? It was our operation. It's over. What's the interest? It's personal. It's my method. It's private.
(*He looks at her to close the subject.*)

SANDRA: And have you heard McKinnon is going to appeal?
(BARRY *smiles, relieved at the change of subject and at once able to relax.*)

BARRY: Oh, sure, yeah . . .

SANDRA: What do you think?

BARRY: I think, why shouldn't he? He'll try and get his sentence cut. Fair enough. He's learnt pretty fast. He'll play the system. He'll have his go. That's the game.

SANDRA: Do you think he's got a chance?

BARRY: Why are you asking me? It's not in my hands. (*He is suddenly firm, as if his patience were worn down.*) Yes, I mean *no*, since you ask me. To be honest, he shouldn't be in prison. But then none of them should. Because it isn't a deterrent. He shouldn't be in prison because prison doesn't work. I'd dye them. No really. I mean it. The colour according to what they're found to have done. Give them red hands for a burglary. If it's a sex offence, paint their heads green. There should be a code, so we all know. So we can all laugh at them when they walk down the street. (*He shakes his head.*) I'm serious, Sandra.

SANDRA: I know you are. (*She looks at him a moment, reacting to his ill temper.*) There was this woman once. I was on traffic duty. I'd had twenty-ton lorries pushing smoke up my nostrils all day. She was half into a bus lane. I was pretty

70

foul to her, nothing excessive, I was cutting, I was just short. You know what she said? 'Jesus, you've all got so touchy. Talking to the police is like dealing with an ethnic minority.'

(BARRY *turns away, really irritated by this story.*)

BARRY: Oh, sure, hell, what does she know?

SANDRA: You've got to fight it, Barry.

BARRY: Don't tell *me* to fight it.

SANDRA: You're getting ratty as hell. You're getting like the others. You know that.

BARRY: Oh, and you aren't? (*He turns away, furious, but laughing at her now.*) Oh, of course not, you're on the way *up*, I forgot. You're doing the *exams*. You'll get a Toblerone to put on your desk, with your name on it, you'll get the braid, the only problem is . . . (*He stops a moment, smiling, sure of his point.*) Did anyone mention this? What comes with promotion? Did anyone *say*?

SANDRA: What?

(*He smiles, infuriating.*)

What?

BARRY: Did no one tell you? It comes with the car and the pension. You have to buy into the bullshit as well.

SANDRA: Oh, really?

BARRY: Yeah. (*He moves a little towards her, triumphant.*) If you stay where I am, if you stick in the ranks, if you're just a grunt in the canteen, well, we may be low, but we do have one big advantage. We don't have to pretend that everything is great.

(*They are now opposite each other.* SANDRA *is holding down her anger.*)

SANDRA: Well, of course, I don't have your experience. No one beats you for that, Barry. You're our man on the street. Everyone's favourite policeman. Totally competent. And totally paranoid. (*She stops suddenly, a change in her tone.*) I've been trying to find out just why that is.

(BARRY *watches her dispassionately.*)

71

I took out the file. Yeah. On the Fielding case. Something bothered me. You sent the boy out. In the flat, you sent McKinnon away. _—reveals to Barry_

BARRY: Did I?

SANDRA: I know. I was there. But you lied about that at the trial. (*She lifts it up.*) And you talked alone with the two who already knew you. (*She waits.*) Why? Why did you do that?

BARRY: Sandra, it's over. It's dead. Nobody's interested.
(*Suddenly* TOBY *has appeared and the atmosphere has to change.*)
At least no one was until now. Hello, Toby.

TOBY: Hello, Barry. You haven't seen Lester?
(BARRY *walks casually away from* SANDRA, *trying to seem at ease.*)

SANDRA: Yeah, he's in with the immigrants.

TOBY: I've got to go and get a bail-jumper.
(BARRY *laughs.*)

BARRY: Spare us, Toby, it's one o'clock.

TOBY: Yeah, I know, but I've never had one before.

BARRY: Yeah, well, he's out there.

TOBY: Thanks. I'll get my body. I'll be back in a mo.
(*He goes out through the main charge-room door to the outside.*
BARRY *has picked up his cup and is smiling.* SANDRA *is reasonable, gentle.*)

SANDRA: I'm not threatening you, Barry. Why should I want to? (*She smiles.*) It's just if you look at it . . . I mean, only for a moment . . . if you were to look at it from my point of view. It's true. I'm a high-flyer, as everyone keeps telling me. They've chosen me. I'm going up. But that shouldn't mean being taken for an idiot. That feeling's not good. I tell you, you wouldn't like it. Does going up mean you turn a blind eye? (*She shakes her head.*) Because if that's it, it's buying into a nightmare. It makes everything a lie. Yeah, go up, head on up. But turn your face away from what's going on below you. Turn into a spaghetti-head.

72

Meaning: just keep out of it. Pretend nothing's happening. (*She looks down.*) I'm sorry. But I want to find out.

(*He looks at her a moment.*)

BARRY: You know, when I was a kid, I used to go to the pictures. Nearly every week there was usually this guy. He was the hero. Why was he the hero? Because he was the one who said no . . . (*He looks up to check she recognizes this.*) Remember? He always had this kind of certainty. There was always some scandal, or some sort of scam going on. And this bloke'd get up and he'd say, 'I don't care what any of you think of me, but I have to tell you: I think this is wrong.' And all the others would look kind of shifty, and he'd say, 'I don't care, I don't care what you think. OK, I'm out on my own. But there's something more important than any of us. Yes, you see, there's a *principle* here . . .' (*He smiles.*) And I used to think, now why exactly am I meant to like this geezer? I know I'm meant to say, 'Wow what a guy!' But I don't. (*He turns now and looks at* SANDRA, *sure of his point.*) And *you* don't actually, Sandra, all your instincts are exactly like mine . . .

(*She shifts, uneasy.*)

SANDRA: I'm not sure what you mean.

BARRY: I mean I didn't like him. It's all so easy. 'Let me show you my conscience . . .' That's the easy way. The hard way's the other one, the one that's taken by all the poor bloody foot soldiers, like Lester and Jimmy and Dave . . . (*He gestures offstage.*) Who'd never even think of betraying their pals. But they have a talent which no one seems to value. Their talent is for turning up every day. (*He nods.*) Yeah. For being there. And, OK, there's a lot of moaning, they moan in the canteen, they whinge, they complain about the job. But they keep on doing it. And all the shit is landed in their laps. And nobody thanks them. No, on the contrary, it's all directives, it's supervision, it's

73

behavioural correction courses, it's 'Did I hear you make a sexist remark . . .?' (*He gets up, acting out the questions*.) It's 'Are you racist? Are you foul-mouthed? Do you never lose your temper? Do you censor your speech?' Do you put up with all this, all day, day in, day out? Being treated on sufferance? Being scapegoats for everything that goes wrong. 'Oh, there's a traffic jam. There's a drug epidemic. Crime's on the increase. The young have no respect any more. We're not free to demonstrate. We're not allowed to strike.' (*He stops*.) '*I didn't win the pools last week.*' (*He turns savagely towards her*.) 'Hey, wait a moment, tell you what . . . *let's blame the police . . .*' (*But* SANDRA *is not giving way*.)

SANDRA: What are you saying? That we're all beyond criticism?

BARRY: No. No, I'm not saying that. I'm saying, you stand there, Sandra, you tell stories about how we're all getting touchy. *Touchy?* Really? You're *touchy?* When people say everything's your fault? I can't think why. Surely you can take twenty-four-hour round-the-clock criticism and learn not to react? (*He stops, suddenly quietening to make his point*.) Well, actually you can. By dissembling. That's how you do it. By being secret. By doing things your way. (*He smiles*.) Yes, a copper is allowed something. It's all he's got. You're allowed a few private moments with criminals. You're allowed a way of doing things which is actually your own.

(SANDRA's *gaze does not waver. She is quiet when she speaks, not accusing*.)

SANDRA: You mean you're bent?

(*There is a silence*. BARRY *is so angry at the question that his reply comes out as politeness, ice cold*.)

BARRY: I'm sorry?

SANDRA: You mean those men are innocent?

(*Again he pauses, to repress his anger*.)

BARRY: No. How can they be? We found the goods.

74

SANDRA: If they're guilty, then why are you so defensive?

BARRY: The obvious reason. I don't think I've done anything wrong. (*He looks at her a moment.*) I went in there, all right. I knew this gang of old. I thought, right, this is it. This is what you wait for. So . . . yes . . . I came out with my bag.

SANDRA: Bag?

BARRY: I did my trick. It always works.

SANDRA: What sort of trick?

(*There is a pause. He is quite still.*)

BARRY: I carry dynamite. I carry sticks of dynamite. Semtex, actually. I keep it at home. It works pretty well. It's always worked well for me. People never quite know. Once they see it, they stop thinking clearly. Especially if they're from over the sea . . .

(SANDRA *is still now.*)

SANDRA: I saw them.

BARRY: That's right. Yes, you did.

SANDRA: At your place. In the fridge. I didn't think. In a packet. You told me it was wax for the kid.

BARRY: (*Smiles*) It may be wax. Or it may not be. Excuse me, Sandra, but that's the whole point. (*He is suddenly insistent.*) It's about acting, it's about credibility, Sandra, it's about going nuts. They have to believe that you are a complete bloody fruitcake. (*He is nodding.*) You've never seen it but I've got a good act.

SANDRA: Yes, I'm sure.

BARRY: You have to convince them. I said, you're both going down for six years. Well, you'll get another five, now this has been found on the premises. How do you like that? You got it. Unless . . .

SANDRA: Unless? Unless what?

BARRY: (*Shakes his head*) Unless what do you think? Christ almighty, what is our trade? What is our living? You're a policeman. What is your oxygen? You need information. (*He turns, suddenly acting it out.*) 'Give me information, you shits . . .'

75

SANDRA: And they did?

(*He laughs with excitement.*)

BARRY: Oh yes. So three weeks later in the City of London when some Mick bullion robbers – Kilmartin? Remember? Yes, you read about it – on the front page – when Kilmartin and his gang turned up at the bank, thanks to that little package I showed Travis and Fielding, the Flying Squad was waiting! Bang! Double bubble! Two lots of villains. Both gangs very nasty, very nasty people. No sweat. (*He nods, pleased with this.*) And, what's more, I'm up for the Commissioner's medal.

(*But before he has even said this,* SANDRA *has moved away slowly across the room.*)

SANDRA: Barry, you're out of your mind.

BARRY: Sandra, Kilmartin's gang had shotguns.

SANDRA: So?

BARRY: Which they would have used.

SANDRA: That doesn't make it *right*.

BARRY: Only they didn't. Because, thank Christ, I managed to forestall them. (*He turns and looks at her.*) Can you please tell me why stopping that happening is *bad*?

(*But* SANDRA *is holding her ground.*)

SANDRA: I think you know it is.

BARRY: Oh, do I?

SANDRA: Of course. What you've got is an unsafe prosecution. It's crazy. If you'd been caught, you'd have lost the lot. You'd have lost everything. You still could.

BARRY: I don't know what you mean by 'If I'd been caught'. (*He looks at her a moment.*) Sandra, these people are scum. We're dealing with scum. And we're not being given the power we need to deal with them. A policeman without power, that's a contradiction. They're sending us out with *nothing* these days. So we each have to make it. You make your own stick of dynamite. And then you use it.

SANDRA: It isn't right, Barry.

(*He turns and looks at her, calmly contemptuous.*)

76

BARRY: Oh, really, is that what you think?

SANDRA: Yes, it is. (*She looks at him unforgivingly.*) It's just stupid, it's bloody stupid. That's the thing about you, Barry, you used to be smart. You were really smart. Until your main interest got to be in beating the system. Working out your grievance. And that's when you began to get really dumb. Because you lose sight of things. You're so concerned to do it your way, to prove you're the guy who's got it over everyone else, you lose sight of what the point is. We're meant to make sure that the criminals go down.

BARRY: They've gone down.

SANDRA: Sure. But they've gone down the crappy way. Because at some time, at some point, someone will notice. They'll spot you, Barry. I know it. And maybe it's a good thing they do.

BARRY: Why's that?

SANDRA: Because you're a danger. You are. Your brain's somewhere else. It's not on the job. It's on the aggravation. All right, I know, for God's sake, it gets to me too. But I used to admire you, Barry.

(*Her voice breaks. She is overwhelmed for a moment.*)

BARRY: Then, OK, that's fine. Please. Go tell the Chief Super. If it 'worries' you, then OK, go ahead. Please. Be Gary Cooper. Be any bloody movie actor you like. What the world needs now is another prima donna. Parade your conscience. But all you'll do is make yourself despised by a lot of decent people. And that's not the clever thing it is in the films. It's long. And it's nasty. And what's worst, it's selfish, because we all know it's really about showing off. (*He turns from across the room.*) You can do that. Death or glory. Do it. You're welcome, Sandra. But no one will ever trust you again. (*He smiles.*) 'Shut up, here comes Sandra. Don't tell Sandra. Say nothing, Sandra's around.' Perhaps that's what you want.

(SANDRA *doesn't answer. From outside the charge-room door*

77

the sudden noise of struggle, pitched loud and violent.)
Me, I stopped going to the movies. Let's hear it for the
guys who keep turning up.
(*The charge-room door is thrown open.* TOBY *comes bursting
through it, locked in the arms of a wild drunk in his fifties,
really filthy and fighting mad, known as* NELSON. *They are
already scrapping, so they fall together on to the desk, both
shouting.*)
TOBY: Jesus Christ, get hold of him, bloody hell, what's
happening?
SANDRA: Lester!
NELSON: I've had enough of this bloody bastard.
(LESTER *at once appears from the front.*)
LESTER: Now watch it, go easy, what the hell is this?
(TOBY *has struggled free of* NELSON, *who is sprawled across
Lester's desk.*)
TOBY: This dickhead has just been sick on my shoes.
NELSON: You're all bloody bastards. I hate the lot of you.
(TOBY *starts to pull him off the desk but nobody makes any
attempt to help.* LESTER *simply moves round to go and sit
down in his place.*)
LESTER: Oh, right, yes . . .
NELSON: I hate the bloody sodding police.
LESTER: Why can't they get a new tune? We've heard it.
(*He suddenly turns round and, from nowhere, shouts at*
NELSON, *who is being messily armlocked by* TOBY.)
Do you have any idea, you stupid arsehole, how bloody
boring it is for us?
(NELSON *makes a wild attempt at a punch.* TOBY *is just
managing to hold it together but* LESTER *just watches.*)
Hold him. Hold the stupid bugger. Please, Toby, come
on. Page one. Delivering a body. Please deliver a body in
reasonable shape.
(TOBY *has him straight now and under control.* BARRY *has
wandered a few paces away, just watching.* SANDRA *is not
moving, still where she was. And now* ESTHER *has appeared*

78

from the front, hearing the commotion.)

TOBY: I'm sorry, Sarge.

LESTER: Your hat is crooked.

TOBY: My bollocks are crooked as well.

(LESTER *doesn't look up, just shouts.*)

LESTER: Esther!

ESTHER: Yeah?

LESTER: Go and rehang Toby's bollocks.

ESTHER: I know how to do that. I did the course.

(*Suddenly* BARRY *speaks, dangerous, quiet.*)

BARRY: Why not ask Sandra? She's a hands-on police officer.
She'll always pitch in. She's always there for you.
(*He suddenly looks across the room at her. After all the noise,
there is a sudden silence.*)
Aren't you? You can trust Sandra.
(*He looks at her a moment, then turns and walks straight out
of the room.*)
Tell Jimmy I had to go home.
(*He's gone.* LESTER *does not look up from writing.* ESTHER *is
anxiously looking across the room to* SANDRA.)

LESTER: Oh blimey-deary, did I miss something?

ESTHER: I think Barry's got his period.

LESTER: Yeah, that's what it is.
(NELSON *has gone to sit down on the bench and* TOBY *is
standing near him.* ESTHER *walks casually by* SANDRA.)

ESTHER: (*With a tone of real concern*) You all right, sweetheart?
(NELSON *yells before* SANDRA *can answer.*)

NELSON: You're all bloody bastards.

LESTER: Will you shut up?
(LESTER *has still not looked up.*)

SANDRA: I'm fine, I'm back on, no worries.

LESTER: Will you do a minor accident? In the Clapham Road?
Esther, you go along too.
(SANDRA *goes to take the piece of paper he is holding up.*
LESTER *looks up a second.*)
You all right really?

79

SANDRA: Sure.

(*She goes to get her jacket and puts it on.* ESTHER *goes to get hers.* LESTER *writes.* NELSON *subsides.* TOBY *dreams. Sudden peace. It's the schoolroom again.* SANDRA *picks up her hat, and on the way out speaks half to herself and half to the room.*)

No problem. I'm one of the boys.

[handwritten: — Given in, Not going to tell on Barry]

SCENE FOUR

As SANDRA *goes we move to the shower block of the prison. In the main room, which we do not see clearly and which is suggested only by its dim outline and, more importantly, by the sound of the water jets, there are thirty or forty shower heads in the communal bathing area. At the front,* GERARD *appears, wet from the showers, with a towel wrapped round him. He is about to dry himself when another* PRISONER *appears beside him. He is older, tattooed and still wet.*

FIRST PRISONER: You see, it's just this.

(GERARD *turns.*)

GERARD: I'm sorry?

FIRST PRISONER: It's this. It's just this.

(GERARD *looks and sees a* SECOND PRISONER *has appeared. He is younger, crew-cut and powerfully built.*)

We need you to do something for us.

GERARD: Something for you?

FIRST PRISONER: That's right.

(GERARD *eyes them a moment.*)

GERARD: I've got to go.

FIRST PRISONER: No. You're doing something for us.

GERARD: What's that?

(*The two* PRISONERS *don't answer, they just stand right by him.*)

Can I go?

FIRST PRISONER: No.

GERARD: What do you want me to do?

SECOND PRISONER: You've got to take your towel off. You've got to live life with no towel.

(*There is a moment.* GERARD *takes one step back and looks to the opening that leads to the shower room.*)

FIRST PRISONER: Don't call for a screw. There isn't one.

SECOND PRISONER: There is one. He's not coming, though.

FIRST PRISONER: There's more of us.

(GERARD *again looks to the gap.*)

There's two on the door.

(GERARD *waits a moment.*)

GERARD: Then what is this?

FIRST PRISONER: You've seen a black bitch.

GERARD: I'm sorry?

FIRST PRISONER: You see a black lawyer bitch, that's what they say. (*He turns to the* SECOND PRISONER.) Turn the showers up, will you?

(*The* SECOND PRISONER *goes out to the main room.*)

I like the noise.

(GERARD *looks as if he might try to make a run for it.*)

You know what smart people do?

(*The sound of the showers being turned up, hotter and harder.* GERARD *doesn't answer.*)

They do their time, Gerard. They do it. They just do it. (*He waits a moment.*) They never put themselves first.

(GERARD *is shaking now. The* FIRST PRISONER *moves closer to him.*)

Wherever you go, we can get to you. Don't ever think there's anywhere safe.

(*The* SECOND PRISONER *has reappeared in the opening.*)

SECOND PRISONER: Has he taken his towel off?

FIRST PRISONER: Not yet.

(*The* FIRST PRISONER *moves right up to* GERARD *and gently reaches out to take the top of the towel around* GERARD's *waist, as if to rip it off.*)

We want it off because we don't want blood on it.

SECOND PRISONER: You can wipe up afterwards with this.
(*The* SECOND PRISONER *has moved towards him and now throws him a rag he has had in his hand. The* FIRST PRISONER *still has his hand on the waist of* GERARD'S *towel.*)
FIRST PRISONER: Is that all right?
(GERARD *cannot answer. The stage begins to darken. The* SECOND PRISONER *walks round behind* GERARD *to put his arm round* GERARD'S *neck. The sound of the showers, hotter still and louder.*)
Take him to the showers, and let's get to work.
(*As* GERARD *is seized by the* SECOND PRISONER *and pulled backwards towards the opening, the sound of the showers drowns out his screaming, and the lights lose them as they go.*)

SCENE FIVE

Outside the chambers. At once, as GERARD *is dragged off,* IRINA *appears, distraught, tired-looking. As the prison disappears, she sees a group of men all laughing together in a clubby way, all clerks to the lawyers, standing together in suits.*

IRINA: Oh, Woody, there you are, I've been trying to find you.
(*At once* WOODY *turns from out of the group, sees it's* IRINA, *and detaches himself from it, winking at the others as if at some hidden joke.*)
WOODY: See you later, lads.
ALL: See you, Woody.
(*He walks across to join* IRINA *and they head for the chambers. The group on the lawn disperses as they go.*)
WOODY: Yeah, I'm sorry. I've been out getting work.
(*He indicates a bundle of briefs under his arm.*)
IRINA: It's just I needed an appointment for a word with Sir Peter. I've been trying for days.
WOODY: Well, you're never here.

82

IRINA: No.

WOODY: Running round the country. Thanks to all my efforts on your behalf.

(IRINA *smiles, taking this lightly.*)

How is it out there?

IRINA: Oh, it's great.

WOODY: Are you sure? You look shattered. Is it all getting to you?

IRINA: What?

WOODY: I mean the job.

(*She stops, frowning.*)

IRINA: Did someone say that?

WOODY: No. (WOODY *looks puzzled, as if not understanding her concern.*) No, of course not. I'm joking, that's all.

(*They go into Sir Peter's chambers in Lincoln's Inn, white-panelled, with Georgian prints on the walls, and all the comforts of his profession, the fine desk, the books, the lamps.* WOODY *sets about sorting his papers.*)

No, on the contrary, that's not the word on you.

IRINA: Oh, what's the word, then?

WOODY: You know as well as I do. (*He grins. His tone is very light.*) You're very popular. Sir Peter adores you.

IRINA: Yes, Woody, I know.

(WOODY *does not notice how guarded her tone is as he arranges stuff on the desk.*)

WOODY: He was really excited, you should have heard him, he kept telling me, it was what he was praying for. You were eating at the Ritz . . .

IRINA: Yes.

(*She waits, not getting the point of* WOODY's *pleasure in this.*)

So?

WOODY: Then Toppy Pilkington came in?

IRINA: That's right.

(*She frowns.* WOODY *is grinning delightedly.*)

Well?

WOODY: You see, they're old rivals. Deadly!

83

IRINA: Rivals?

WOODY: Just in the libel court, that's all I mean.

(WOODY *smiles. She looks uncomprehending.*)

He said you should have seen Toppy's expression. When he saw Sir Peter with you, at a table for two. Toppy could barely choke down his Lobster Thermidor.

(IRINA *frowns, interrupting.*)

IRINA: Woody, it's only appearances.

WOODY: Sure. I know that. (*He throws her a quick glance.*) No problem.

IRINA: You do understand that?

(*He still has a smile on his face as he works. Then he looks up to find she is still looking at him.*)

WOODY: Hey, lighten up. You need a sense of humour.

IRINA: That's what Sir Peter says.

(WOODY *looks at her a moment.*)

WOODY: It's a fine balance. You know that, Miss Platt. He's not a fool. He wouldn't have had you as his junior unless you could argue a case. But also . . . (*He's quieter.*) Let's face it, you've got to play a slightly tricky game. And there's one way to do that.

IRINA: Is there? (*She looks at him, impassive.*) How's that?

WOODY: Gracefully, Irina. Do it with a smile on your face.

(*And at once* SIR PETER *appears, in full fig, unloading his papers and starting to take off his wig and gown.*)

And now here's Sir Peter . . .

SIR PETER: Good morning, everyone.

WOODY: I'm sorry, I should have carried your gear.

(WOODY, *like a manservant, has gone into the ritual of gathering Sir Peter's clothes and papers.* SIR PETER *smiles at* IRINA.)

SIR PETER: Irina.

IRINA: Peter. Did you have a good morning in court?

SIR PETER: Certainly. Chancery. Such a relief after criminals.

(*He turns, smiling at her.*) You know what's so boring about criminal law?

84

IRINA: I think I can guess.

SIR PETER: Go on.

IRINA: It involves real human beings.

(SIR PETER *smiles and gestures assent*.)

SIR PETER: That's one disadvantage. But also you have to establish the facts.

(WOODY *has gone round to open a bottle of beer*.)

That's why I also like libel cases. Because so often they're a matter of opinion. You're arguing about things which no one can prove. You're juggling with air, pure and simple. (*He smiles at* IRINA.) And these are the cases where I seem to do well.

WOODY: I can't think why.

(WOODY *offers him a drink*.)

Your glass of beer?

SIR PETER: Yes, thank you.

(*At his desk*, SIR PETER *flicks a look up to* IRINA, *sensing already she is not susceptible to his good cheer*.)

IRINA: Our man's been beaten up.

WOODY: Yes, Woody mentioned.

(*He looks at once to* WOODY, *who is pouring himself a glass*.)

IRINA: He's put himself on Rule 43.

SIR PETER: Very wise.

IRINA: I've seen him. The regime is appalling. He's often banged up for twenty-three hours a day.

SIR PETER: What did I tell you? Bloody criminal law!

WOODY: You said it.

(IRINA *tries not to be put off*.)

IRINA: Yes, but in fact, as far as the case goes, the actual beating up is good news for us. It vindicates McKinnon.

SIR PETER: Do you think?

IRINA: It proves that Travis and Fielding are frightened. They attack him because they've got so much to hide.

(SIR PETER *frowns, holding back*.)

SIR PETER: Do they?

IRINA: I'd have thought it was obvious. They're police

85

informers. Aren't they? You said that yourself.

SIR PETER: I said they could be.

IRINA: They did some sort of deal under pressure. Now
plainly they're scared. If McKinnon speaks up, they're
identified. They're in trouble with whoever they shopped.
(*She smiles as if it's QED, but* SIR PETER *is not moved.*)

SIR PETER: Irina, my dear, it was a fight in prison. Have you
ever been in prison?

IRINA: Of course.

SIR PETER: I've known people fight over half an ounce of
tobacco. They fight when they dislike the look on
someone's face. (*He shakes his head.*) Are you telling me –
without any friendly witnesses – you can establish that
this fight had one particular cause? (*He turns aside,
suddenly passionate.*) And here again – here we go! – my
God, do I have *déjà vu?* – *once again* in this case, it's on the
word of one man. Which man? The same man.
(IRINA *is shaking her head, disbelieving.*)
And, *once again*, there's no actual proof.
(*He has leant forward.* IRINA *can't wait to interrupt.*)

IRINA: You don't understand. Gerard says . . .

SIR PETER: I know what Gerard *says*, but has it not occurred
to you – be serious, please – Irina, this is actually the
twenty-eighth day . . .

IRINA: You think I don't know?

SIR PETER: Today we have to lodge our grounds for appeal.
(WOODY *chips in, respectfully.*)

WOODY: I was going to remind you.

SIR PETER: Thank you, Woody. And you want us to argue all
these convictions are unsafe on the grounds of one wild
allegation by one proven liar about a policeman's dolly-
bag of plastic supposed explosive which no one else
remembers seeing at all?
(IRINA *is shaking her head.*)
Whereas, on the other hand – please let me finish – I can
enter a perfectly decent appeal against sentence, far easier,

86

far simpler, what we might call the 'lame-dog' appeal. Meaning: the poor bastard is young, he's got a wife and two children, one of them, I gather, imperfect, it's his first offence. So, on sentimental grounds, his sentence must be cut.

IRINA: I know. (*She hesitates, uneasy now.*) I know you can do that.

SIR PETER: If we go for a lesser sentence, we've got a good chance. (*He suddenly points an accusing finger at her.*) But, of course – now we get to it – you don't want to do that. You're not happy with that. Of course! Irina is not happy. Why not?

(*She looks at him resentfully, trapped.*)

Come on, spit it out. Don't be ashamed. We all know you're thinking it, you might as well say it. Enlighten us.

IRINA: I don't want to do it because it isn't right.

(SIR PETER *turns at once, vindicated.*)

SIR PETER: Ah well, there we are, I knew it . . .

IRINA: The police were on the fiddle!

SIR PETER: That's what you think. I don't need to tell you, that isn't our business. We've only one duty and that's to our client. (*He sits back, exasperated.*) I mean, just look at it, examine it objectively, say we decided, all right, something funny's gone on . . .

IRINA: It has.

SIR PETER: So what's the next step? We apply to the Registrar of Appeals – always assuming he's amenable – for funds to hire a private detective. Even if we get them – and that's a big if – just think. This inquiry agent – some dumb Joe – he's got a very nice job. He's got to walk up the steps of a South London police station and go up to the six-foot hairy ape on the counter and say, 'Hold on, I wonder, could you help me? I think something fishy may have gone on round here.'

(*He laughs.*)

WOODY: It doesn't sound a good way to make a living.

87

SIR PETER: Do you really think our man's got a chance? With an experienced detective like Barry Hopper?

IRINA: Hopper's got a sidekick.

SIR PETER: I know.

IRINA: He's not impossible. I saw something there. (*She turns, improvising.*) And that policewoman. I watched her at the trial. Now she's a human being.

(SIR PETER *is shaking his head.*)

SIR PETER: Irina, you have been my dinner date. You simply cannot be this naïve. (*He is up now, pouring more beer.*) It's called a force. Police *force*, that's the name for it. Everyone knows. It's the wrong word. If I could pass an Act of Parliament, I'd call it what it actually is. (*He smiles.*) 'Club'. Police club. And, unless you find someone who's interested in jacking in their membership, you haven't got a cat's chance in hell.

(IRINA *is looking at him now, as if understanding what has been bothering her.*)

IRINA: You don't believe him.

(SIR PETER *is caught off balance.*)

SIR PETER: I'm sorry?

IRINA: You don't believe what Gerard says.

SIR PETER: That hardly matters.

IRINA: You think he's lying.

(SIR PETER *looks at her, firm again.*)

SIR PETER: He's fighting for his life. Since you ask, yes, I think he has a technique. Maximum confusion. He's decided that's his best chance. He lied in court. We know that. Persistently. Now those lies are all bust. So. The next stage is unfounded allegation. It's not an unfamiliar route. Discredit the police. Discredit the prison staff. Engineer an attack. Claim you're a victim. (*He stops and looks at her.*) Then find someone who'll swallow it whole.

(IRINA *is quiet now, attentive.*)

IRINA: Someone?

SIR PETER: Yes.

88

IRINA: You mean me?

   (SIR PETER *just smiles*.)

   So you think he just leads me by the nose?

SIR PETER: No. I don't think it's your nose he's got you by. (*There is a sudden silence as if they can't quite believe what they've heard.* WOODY *shifts.*)

WOODY: I think this may be my moment to go.

IRINA: No, Woody, don't go . . .

   (WOODY *hovers a moment, uncertain, between them.*)

SIR PETER: You forget I represented this man. I know him. I've represented dozens of people like him.

IRINA: *Like* him?

SIR PETER: Certainly. I do know the type.

IRINA: Oh, do you? (*Her anger is low and dangerous.*) What type is that?

SIR PETER: You know perfectly well.

IRINA: No, I don't actually. Tell me.

SIR PETER: He's an ordinary, slightly sub-average human being who has landed himself in a damn stupid mess.

IRINA: Sub-average?

SIR PETER: Of course he's sub-average.

IRINA: How *dare* you say that?

   (SIR PETER *smiles, enjoying himself.*)

SIR PETER: Think about it, Irina. It's not such a terrible thing. I hate to have to tell you, but by definition, sub-average is what half the human race is fated to be.

IRINA: Yes. (*There is suddenly a lethal tone in her voice.*) No doubt. If you think in those terms.

   (*For the first time* SIR PETER *is rattled by her.*)

SIR PETER: Look, for God's sake, it's obvious he's lying . . .

IRINA: Is it?

SIR PETER: Of course. I don't blame him. He's fighting like a rat.

IRINA: How do you *know*?

   (SIR PETER *shakes his head, confident.*)

SIR PETER: How do I know? After a while, you do develop an

instinct. That's one of the things a first-rate advocate has. Your profession, after all, is the judgement of people. It's not even conscious. It becomes animal. It's a gut instinct. Here. (*He points to his heart.*) I'd say if anything it's *the* crucial ability. You're asked to walk every day through a minefield of lies. If nothing else, you do develop a certain forensic capacity for distinguishing invention from truth. (IRINA *has moved away, quiet now, sure of herself.*)

IRINA: The other night . . .

SIR PETER: Yes?

IRINA: When we had dinner . . . you remember, we had dinner at the Ritz? We were waiting for a cab. I said how much I'd enjoyed myself. (SIR PETER *smiles.*)

SIR PETER: You did.

IRINA: What a wonderful evening I'd had. (*She pauses, dangerous.*) Now, please, I'd be interested, answer me forensically, what's your opinion? (*She smiles, hanging the next question in the air.*) You know about these things. Was I telling the truth? (SIR PETER *pauses, looking for the lawyer's answer.*)

SIR PETER: I would have said . . . you appeared to enjoy it.

IRINA: What did I think of *The Magic Flute?*

SIR PETER: You liked it.

IRINA: Did I?

SIR PETER: Of course. You said you did. It's a great opera. (*He hesitates a second, fatally.*) The tickets were extremely expensive.

IRINA: Oh, well, in that case, it isn't in doubt. (*She has spat this remark out so forcefully that* SIR PETER *is shocked.*)

SIR PETER: I don't know what you mean. What do you prove by this?

IRINA: I will tell you. These judgements, these 'judgements' you make all the time, these judgements which seem to be graven in stone, they have only the status of prejudice.

90

SIR PETER: That is really not true.

(IRINA *has wandered away, fired up now*.)

IRINA: Do you not hear it? Do you never notice it? (*She characterizes*.) 'I was talking to *Woody* and he was telling me that *Toppy* was feeling green with jealousy, and *Chugger* no doubt was feeling something else . . .' (*She turns, unable to contain her bewilderment*.) And *I* am feeling . . . did I come all this way to take up residence in the pages of the *Beano*? Am I going crazy? Does no one else see? (*She looks round the room, sure of herself now*.) It seems so obvious to an outsider. Do you really not know? All this behaviour, the honours, the huge sums of money, the buildings, the absurd dressing-up. They do have a purpose. It's anaesthetic. It's to render you incapable of imagining life the other way round.

(SIR PETER *shifts, uncomfortable*.)

SIR PETER: That is simply ridiculous.

IRINA: Is it? (*She smiles*.) Is it? What about the whole joke of you, who claim this infallible instinct for deception, this forensic gift for detecting the truth? You sit there – what? A Knight Commander of the British Empire. (*She laughs*.) You're conspiring in a lie. It's a lie. What British Empire? Hasn't word reached you? It no longer exists.

(SIR PETER *points to her, having no time to censor his reaction*.)

SIR PETER: Now that is actually profoundly offensive.

IRINA: Is it?

SIR PETER: A knighthood is hardly a lie. It's not a lie. It's . . . a form of words.

IRINA: And there's a difference?

SIR PETER: Of course.

(*She shakes her head*.)

IRINA: It seems so clear, you see only what you want to . . .

SIR PETER: That's not true.

IRINA: 'Oh, I don't do criminal law.'

SIR PETER: I don't. (*He shifts, suspecting a trap*.) I don't like it.

91

IRINA: I wonder, what's the reason for that?

SIR PETER: I've said. Intellectually.

IRINA: I'll tell you the reason. When you accept a civil case, it's a clear forty thousand just for taking the brief.

(SIR PETER *turns at once to* WOODY.)

SIR PETER: Have you been disclosing my figures?

WOODY: No.

IRINA: Plus your refreshers. Fifteen hundred a day. (*She laughs, enjoying herself.*) The intellectual attractions of civil law become suddenly apparent.

(SIR PETER *is at once vehement.*)

SIR PETER: It makes absolutely no difference. I bring the same skills and attitudes, whatever I'm paid.

IRINA: Do you? (*She looks at him.*) Do you really? Woody said, before I insisted, you had decided in McKinnon's case not even to appeal. On *any* grounds.

(SIR PETER *swings round on* WOODY *at once.*)

SIR PETER: Did you tell her that?

WOODY: Well, no, I . . .

IRINA: Hold on, Woody.

SIR PETER: No, let's get this clear.

(WOODY *pauses, hating this situation.*)

WOODY: I hinted at it. I thought that was fair.

SIR PETER: Woody, I'm shocked at you.

IRINA: Please, Woody isn't the issue. Is it true you were going to let the whole sentence stand?

(SIR PETER *is calm now.*)

SIR PETER: Yes. Yes, since you ask me. (*He stops, unapologetic.*) The case was not interesting.

IRINA: Not interesting to *you*.

SIR PETER: It had no distinguishing features. There was no pressure from his solicitor . . .

IRINA: Well, no, there wouldn't be.

SIR PETER: And I was satisfied I'd done what I could.

(*He looks up at her. She is level, serious.*)

IRINA: I attended the trial, remember?

92

SIR PETER: So?

IRINA: I watched you at work. You stumbled over their names. You even called your own client McPherson at one point.

SIR PETER: Irina, I was given the brief overnight. That happens. Three-quarters of all criminal briefs are returned the night before a trial. Because a barrister becomes unavailable.

IRINA: And the law, of course, must be run at the profession's convenience.

(SIR PETER *suddenly flares at this*.)

SIR PETER: So what are you saying? Did I let him down?

IRINA: You'd have just let him *rot*.

(SIR PETER *nods, defiant*.)

SIR PETER: Of course. Because I'm not a crusader. It's not in the brief. Nor should it be. We shouldn't be . . . soggily compassionate about every petty larcenist we're hired to represent. Indeed it's actually dangerous. Because the fact is . . . your judgement goes. As yours is going, Irina. (*He looks at her, beady now.*) There is a glass screen. And our clients, I'm afraid, live on one side of it. We on the other. And much as you may wish it, we cannot break through.

(IRINA *turns to* WOODY, *who is just watching from the side*.)

IRINA: Woody, this appeal we're discussing, which seems to us so urgent, tell us, when will it be heard?

WOODY: Twelve months.

IRINA: Yes.

WOODY: Maybe ten if we're lucky.

IRINA: When the judges are ready. What state will Gerard be in by then?

(SIR PETER *watches, not answering now*.)

Oh yes, every one of us, we all feel self-righteous, we all say what *we* do is fine . . . (*She stops.*) And meanwhile we're losing him. I know. I go in there. I'm watching him vanish. And each person says, 'Oh, you mustn't blame me . . .'

93

(*The room is silent now, a bridge crossed, as if* SIR PETER *at last hears her.*)
But it isn't quite true. Well, is it? You've just told me. You could have done more. Couldn't you? (*She waits.*) Couldn't you?
(SIR PETER *nods slightly.*)

SIR PETER: Yes. And now I shall.
(*She smiles at the lawyer's answer.*)
I took you in. I gave you a tenancy. There are thousands of young counsel who'd kill for the chance . . . (*He looks at her, some tenderness apparent.*) I've always been kind.

IRINA: Yes. I know that. Your gift is for making me aware of that. (*She smiles.*) I am conscious . . . it's in your power to be kind. At every meal. Throughout every opera. In the morning when I come in. At your wish. By your permission. (*She looks at him.*) It's hard to say thank you ten times a day. Because the effort is finally demeaning. I hardly remember, but I was five when my father died. (*She thinks a moment.*) So I've got on without one. I don't need another. Not now. No, thank you.
(*She gets up and starts to walk out of the room. She is quite calm. She smiles at* WOODY *as she goes out.*)
I hope that was graceful enough.

SCENE SIX

Crystal Palace. IRINA *is standing at the top of the hill, right by the great radio mast. She is slightly hidden. Below her, London is laid out, glimmering at dusk on a summer evening. The wind is blowing gently, the air is light. Then* SANDRA *appears in blue jeans and a blouson, walking through the park.* IRINA *steps out where* SANDRA *can see her.* SANDRA *stops.*

IRINA: No, it's not chance.
(SANDRA *looks at her a moment.*)

94

SANDRA: What's this?

    (IRINA *doesn't answer.*)

    I know who you are. I saw you . . .

IRINA: Yes.

SANDRA: At the trial. I don't have to talk to you.

IRINA: No.

SANDRA: It's against the rules.

IRINA: Well, loosely. Technically, yes.

    (IRINA *waits to see if* SANDRA *will go on.*)

SANDRA: You know I can shop you. — criminal Jargon

IRINA: Sure. I'm aware of that.

SANDRA: Improper approaches. Lawyers Jargon.

IRINA: I've not said a thing.

SANDRA: Not yet.

IRINA: I don't think you'd shop me.

SANDRA: Wouldn't I?

IRINA: No.

SANDRA: Why not? You've chosen a woman. Does that make
    you feel safer? Why didn't you choose Jimmy? Or Barry?
    You thought I'd be easier. I sort of resent that.
    (*For the first time they both smile.*)

IRINA: You're free. You don't have to stay. Irina saw how S reacted with Gerard

    (SANDRA *looks at her a moment, then moves just a few paces
    away to look out over London.* IRINA *waits.*)

    So. Is this where you live?

SANDRA: Near by. Selhurst Park. When I was a kid we walked
    over this hill every week. To watch Crystal Palace.

IRINA: That's the sports team?

SANDRA: Yes. They play football.

IRINA: Ah yes. I've done my best to understand England, but
    some of the nuances pass me right by.

    (SANDRA *smiles at this.*)

SANDRA: Crystal Palace don't have many nuances.

    (*But* IRINA *is not fazed, just going on gently.*)

IRINA: Is football an interest of yours?

SANDRA: It was my Dad. He used to take me. He'd walk over

95

the hill to eat fish and chips. I'd stand outside the pub while he had a couple of lagers. (*She smiles.*) He was trying to bring me up as a boy.

IRINA: Oh dear . . .

SANDRA: No, it was nice. At least when I discovered. I'd kind of taken it for granted I was male. But that made it specially interesting, you know, when I was fourteen or fifteen. And I found out I was a girl.

IRINA: Was your Dad a copper?

SANDRA: Yes.

IRINA: I guessed.

SANDRA: Is it really that obvious?

(*They both laugh.*)

He was great. He had this brilliant idea. That policing was really exciting. He said, you're out on your own. Your own boss. It's you and the public. There's no one to tell you you're getting it wrong. You learn on the job. You learn by doing it. Each time you go out, you start over. It's you and them. (*She stops and thinks a moment.*) He complained. But he never stopped loving it.

IRINA: And is that how you feel?

SANDRA: Oh yeah. It's great while you're doing it. But it's sometimes hard to come home.

(*She gives a slightly nervous glance, her real feelings on show, and* IRINA *picks up on her tone.*)

IRINA: You know why I'm here?

SANDRA: Probably.

IRINA: It's this terrible frustration of knowing something . . . something so wrong has happened and then not being able to find any proof.

(SANDRA *looks at her impassively, not giving anything away.*)

SANDRA: Go on.

IRINA: I know what occurred.

SANDRA: You don't *know*.

IRINA: No. I can guess.

(SANDRA *still doesn't react.*)

96

But I need to find one individual . . . I need a friend inside the police.

SANDRA: Yes. I can see.

(SANDRA *looks at her a moment, then moves slightly away*.)

IRINA: My client got beaten up.

SANDRA: Yes. I heard that.

(*There is a pause,* IRINA *confident she has* SANDRA*'s interest*.)

Why did that happen?

IRINA: To shut him up.

SANDRA: Are you sure? Any witnesses?

(IRINA *shakes her head*.)

Well, then you haven't got a case.

(IRINA *waits, knowing* SANDRA *is hooked*.)

IRINA: I'm in trouble at work because of this. They say it's a quite unexceptional brief. Which it is. To me, that's the point. But they have a way of making you feel a bore and a *bad sport* for wanting the truth of something. Do you know that feeling?

SANDRA: No. Never had it.

(IRINA *smiles*.)

IRINA: You see, when you're training, it's the great cliché. Not a day goes by when they don't mention this. A lawyer should never be emotionally involved.

(SANDRA *frowns*.)

SANDRA: But it's true.

IRINA: Is it?

SANDRA: Sure.

IRINA: To me, it's the alibi. It's the great alibi.

SANDRA: It's being a professional.

IRINA: Is that what it is?

(IRINA *smiles*.)

SANDRA: It's like in the police. I know, I've been through this. You let a lot by. You have to.

IRINA: Do you?

SANDRA: Yeah. Yeah. Certainly. Or else you'd go crazy.

97

(SANDRA *looks at her, unapologetic.* IRINA *is quiet again.*)

IRINA: So how do you choose when it's time to say no?

(SANDRA *looks at her a moment now.* IRINA *makes a slight movement towards her with a card.*)

I've written my number here. In case you want to call me.

SANDRA: Thank you.

IRINA: In case you decided . . . you might change your mind.

(SANDRA *takes the card, not moving yet.*)

I was going to walk out. Yes. At one point. This was just a week or two ago. Then I thought, how exactly will that help my client? And the answer is, not at all.

(SANDRA *is still watching her.*)

I was thinking I should move to radical chambers. There's something they call the alternative Bar. Perhaps it would suit me better.

(*She looks and sees* SANDRA *has a smile on her face.*)

Why are you smiling? What are you smiling at?

(SANDRA *just shakes her head, a real warmth suddenly between the two women.*)

Please tell me.

SANDRA: Because there's nothing called the alternative police.

IRINA: No . . .

(*They both smile together, joined by the thought.*)

No, I know that . . .

SANDRA: There isn't a kind of nice lot who all read the *Guardian* and eat salad for lunch.

(IRINA *smiles.*)

You can't join another lot. Not in my profession. You see, in my line of work there's only one crowd.

(*The two women smile, a little diffident. Then they head off separately, small against the vastness of the evening.*)

IRINA: Goodbye, Sandra. Good luck.

SCENE SEVEN

As SANDRA *goes, the court assembles. The High Court. There are fewer people than for the original trial –* COUNSEL *on either side, ushers, the clerks, and above the scene, on a raised platform, places for the three presiding judges. Light is thrown down from a high, opaque ceiling in a vivid square. The three* HIGH COURT JUDGES *arrive with* CUDDEFORD *at their centre. Before taking his seat* CUDDEFORD *bows to the court, and then to the* COUNSEL, *who bow back. The* JUDGES *sit. At once the* CLERK *makes her announcement.*

CLERK: The case of the Crown versus McKinnon in the Court of Appeal, set down to be heard at two o'clock, Mr Justice Cuddeford presiding.

(CUDDEFORD *nods to the* COUNSEL.)

CUDDEFORD: Counsel.

SIR PETER: My Lords. (*He waits a moment.*) May it please your Lordships, Miss Platt will shortly be joining me to appear for the appellant. My learned friend Mr Bird represents the Crown.

(CUDDEFORD *acknowledges them.*)

CUDDEFORD: We have read the papers in the case. We will listen to any further submission you have.

(SIR PETER *looks round the court.*)

SIR PETER: My Lord, as you will understand, we are not here today to appeal against the verdict. The case was conducted with impeccable fairness by the original trial judge. We have no complaints. Furthermore, we have no reason to fault or question in any way the behaviour of the police.

(*As he says this, the light begins to fade in the courtroom and* BARRY *is seen to get up out of the court and come through the door into the corridor outside. He lights a cigarette as* SIR PETER *is heard to go on.*)

The plea we are making is purely and simply a plea for

99

clemency. We are putting ourselves at the court's mercy, asking you to consider the exceptional pressures of circumstance which caused my client to embark on what I can assure you now will be a short-lived career in crime.

(*Along the corridor, hurrying, comes* IRINA *in wig and gown. Just before she reaches the court's door, she drops a paper, but does not notice.* BARRY, *smoking his cigarette, nods at it.*)

BARRY: You dropped a paper.

IRINA: Thank you.

(*He stands and watches her stoop for it.*)

BARRY: Aren't you a bit late?

IRINA: I had another case. There was a jam on the M40.

BARRY: Working you, are they?

IRINA: And what are you doing here?

(*She has stood up and is now facing him. He carries on smoking.*)

BARRY: Oh. Another case, too. I was just dropping by.

IRINA: To make sure there's no problems? No challenge to the evidence?

(BARRY *looks at her mistrustfully.*)

BARRY: I didn't see any sign of your man.

IRINA: No. He doesn't attend. It's his appeal, but they don't ask him.

BARRY: Yeah. It's a funny old world.

(*He is about to walk away, but she can't resist going on.*)

IRINA: I hear you got a medal.

BARRY: That's right.

IRINA: I know how you got it.

(*He looks at her. Her gaze does not waver.*)

If it's of interest, I know what you did.

(*He gives nothing away.*)

BARRY: Do you?

IRINA: I know you think . . . you think it doesn't matter.

BARRY: Do I?

IRINA: You start cutting corners and you think, what's the harm?

100

BARRY: Do we? (*He smiles.*) God, you must really understand us.

IRINA: It isn't hard, is it?

BARRY: Isn't it?

IRINA: I do understand how policemen's minds work.

BARRY: Do you? From what? From your experience? From your deep experience of doing a filthy, thankless job? You really know? Oh, do you? (*He leans in towards her.*) When was anyone last sick on your wig?

(IRINA *almost loses her temper, suddenly taken away by anger, impulsively reaching out for his arm as he moves away.*)

IRINA: Oh, come on, that's a shitty argument . . .

(BARRY *swings round, suddenly dangerous at being touched on the arm.*)

BARRY: You really want to scrap with me? Do you?

(*She is shocked by his sudden violence.*)

You really want to fight? Do you? Please? Outside. No problem. What is it? Queensberry rules?

IRINA: What's the point? I'm sure you'd pretty soon find a way round them.

(*Now she turns, under control again, and starts to move on to the courtroom. But he calls out to her as she does.*)

BARRY: What do you want? What do you people want? Except to tell other people how to do their jobs? Listen, why don't you go and sit on a committee? Yeah, isn't that the English way? A lot of middle-class people sit on a committee and then tell the yobs what we're all doing wrong? (*He smiles contentedly.*) Yeah. That's it. That's what we'd like. Please. We'd value it. Sure. I think it's the one thing the police really need. More advice. That's it. We love it. We can't get enough. Especially from people who don't do the job.

(IRINA *shakes her head, then moves back across the space to take him on.*)

IRINA: You don't bullshit me. I see right through it. All this bullshit drill-sergeant stuff. It's feeble. (*She suddenly moves towards him.*) You broke the rules. You did. The police have got to do better than that.

(BARRY *smiles.*)

BARRY: You may be right. It's not important. Call me stubborn, or what. But I tell you what, I tell you. I don't take lectures on ethics from lawyers. (*He looks at her, closer now.*) Put your hand on your heart, could you say I was wrong?

(*He breaks into a broad smile.* WOODY *comes out of the court and is standing silently behind* IRINA.)

WOODY: Cuddeford's about to deliver. Miss Platt, you'd better come in.

(BARRY *steps back.*)

BARRY: I've got to be going. I'd love to have a drink with you some time.

IRINA: Any time.

BARRY: Call me up if you like. (*He smiles.*) It's not hard to find me. My name's in the book.

(IRINA *turns and goes back into the court. As she does so, the lights change back to emphasize the court. We pick* CUDDEFORD *up in mid-speech.*)

CUDDEFORD: Sir Peter presents the case of his client with an eloquence which is hard to fault. We are satisfied the prisoner's inexperience, his youth, his gullibility, the tragic circumstances of his young family, all these should weigh heavily, and were not, in our opinion, taken sufficiently into account. For these reasons, we are pleased to say, we have no hesitation in reducing the prisoner's sentence from five years to four and a half.

(*The moment he says this, the stage darkens at once, and before any response comes, the court disperses.*)

SCENE EIGHT

The court disperses, and the stage expands again to the shape it was for Act One Scene Six, when IRINA *first visited the prison. It is*

102

*gloomier than ever, dark, strangely quiet, and absolutely deserted
except for a bunch of officers standing together on a landing, like
sheriffs before a gunfight.* IRINA *walks alongside* BECKETT,
making the same journey she made that first day.

IRINA: It's quiet.
BECKETT: Yes.
IRINA: It's really eerie.
BECKETT: There's a drug search. They're all in their cells.
IRINA: I see.
BECKETT: Each cell's being searched. So no one's allowed out.
    They're all locked up. No exercise, no association.
IRINA: How long's it taking?
BECKETT: Oh, only a day.
    (*In the distance, as they come on to the landing, some men yell
    to one another from behind the bars.*)
IRINA: Still, I heard on the radio you're getting a new prison
    inquiry. You must be pleased.
BECKETT: Miss Platt, the only countries that have decent
    prisons are the ones where the government themselves
    have just been let out.
IRINA: Yes.
    (*They come to* GERARD's *cell. The door is closed.* IRINA *slows
    as she reaches it.*)
    How is he feeling? Has anyone told him?
BECKETT: To be honest, he hasn't asked.
    (*The door is opened.* GERARD *is standing with his back to us,
    completely still, looking up to the window.* BECKETT *goes.*
    IRINA *waits. It is silent.*)
IRINA: Gerard.
    (*He doesn't turn.*)
    Gerard.
    (*And he turns. He stares at her a moment.*)
GERARD: You've come to see me.
IRINA: Yes.
GERARD: What is it you want?

103

IRINA: It's your appeal.

GERARD: Ah, sure. (*He flicks a glance at her.*) Did it happen?

IRINA: Yes. They took off six months.

(*He shows no reaction at all.*)

The whole thing was absolutely outrageous. We thought . . . we thought we could get you much less. We thought we'd do better.

GERARD: I'm sure.

IRINA: It's four and a half. That's what they're giving you.

GERARD: All right. (*He waits again.*) Thank you then. Thanks very much.

(IRINA *stands a moment, a little lost.*)

Barbara's gone. Did you know that?

IRINA: No.

GERARD: Yeah. With the kiddies. To her mother's in Belfast. She couldn't carry on here. Not enough money coming into the house . . .

IRINA: No, well, that happens.

GERARD: On her own in London, no way she could survive.

(IRINA *nods.*)

IRINA: So she can't visit you? Unless they move you?

GERARD: That's not what they do. They don't do that. (*He holds up the book he has in his hand.*) Still, thank God for literature, eh?

(IRINA *looks down.*)

IRINA: I'm sorry, Gerard.

GERARD: Forget it.

(*She smiles.*)

IRINA: I said I'd be your friend. And I will. I'll keep coming. It's something I want. Not to say, 'Oh, we're all in separate compartments . . .'

GERARD: But we are. Aren't we?

IRINA: I'm hoping not. (*She makes a slight move to go.*) Can I bring you some books?

GERARD: I've got books. It's a book on Irish history. I've never been interested. But I'm sort of interested now. (*He moves*

104

to the door of the cell.) When I was brought up, it was always a background. But I laughed it off. It's funny. I wonder why I did that. What I'm saying is . . . I'm not laughing now.
(*He nods.* IRINA *looks down.*)

IRINA: No.

GERARD: Goodbye, Irina.

IRINA: Goodbye, Gerard.
(*She goes. He sits alone on his bed.*)

GERARD: It's like the world's saying we've got a part for you. It's like everyone's saying, there's a part you can play. All right, then. I'll play it. (*He smiles.*) I'll take this role.
(*There is a moment's silence, then very quietly, under the scene the Mozart from the Opera House begins to play again. Gradually different areas of the stage begin to be seen. At the police station* SANDRA *is sitting thinking. Behind her,* LESTER *is talking to* ESTHER.)

LESTER: Have you read this? There's a bloke here, he's accused of having sex with a dolphin. Have you read this, Esther? It's in the paper.

ESTHER: No, I haven't seen it.

LESTER: He was found by two underwater policemen. No, I'm not kidding you, that's what it says.
(*The music is beginning to build. In Sir Peter's chambers, in another part of the stage,* SIR PETER *is greeting* WOODY.)

SIR PETER: Good morning, Woody.

WOODY: Good morning, Sir Peter. I thought you might be looking pretty pleased.

SIR PETER: Oh, you heard?

WOODY: Yesterday. In the Chancery Division. You got one over Toppy.

SIR PETER: I flattened him. Pow. On the mat.

WOODY: That's marvellous.

SIR PETER: His legs went under him. And, let me tell you, he wasn't getting up for the count.

WOODY: That's great, because, also, I tell you . . .

(*As* WOODY *goes into a story, the prison area comes to life, with warders and prisoners starting the morning rituals of slopping out.*)

WARDERS: Slopping out! Slopping out, everyone! Get ready, lads. Slopping out when you're ready!

(*The music is still building as* BARRY *appears, talking to unseen colleagues.*)

BARRY: Good morning, all. I don't think I got the grasp of this. I been up all night. It's way out of order. I mean, I'm trying to understand it, but your expenses system is a bureaucratic world of its own.

(IRINA *stands up nervously in a fifth area and addresses an unseen meeting.*)

IRINA: Good evening, everyone, and welcome to the first meeting of the John Wilkes Society, which, as most of you know, will be a forum for lawyers concerned about the state of our penal system. I'm only sorry there are so few of us here.

(JIMMY *breezes into the charge room.*)

LESTER: Hey, Jimmy, good morning.

JIMMY: Morning, all.

LESTER: There's an educational item I'm reading here. It concerns some of our watery brethren . . .

(ESTHER *is reading the paper over* LESTER's *shoulder.*)

ESTHER: I'd rather have a dolphin than most of the men that I know.

(*And now the Magic Flute overture reaches that same point where it catches fire, and all the areas start to dovetail together.*)

WOODY: These new clients, you know, they just had a panic . . .

IRINA: Our president, even, is on a case in Singapore . . .

BARRY: You see, I got the H4, like you told me . . .

IRINA: And can't be here tonight . . .

WOODY: Just before they were due to start, their bottle went . . .

106

IRINA: And I also have a list of well-wishers . . .

LESTER: There were two coppers in wet suits, I promise
  you . . .

SIR PETER: That's marvellous . . .

BARRY: The H4, you know, like in the regular police, it's fine,
  it gets you into golden time, no problem . . .

IRINA: Who are right behind us . . .

LESTER: I promise you, I'm not kidding . . .

WOODY: They wanted to stop the litigation, but it was too
  late . . .

IRINA: . . . but who can't get to our actual meeting tonight . . .

LESTER: They were positioned under the sea. Here, let me
  read you this . . .
    (*He laughs and adjusts the paper to read from it.* IRINA *gets
    out a piece of paper to read from that.* BARRY *gets out his
    expenses claim.* WOODY *starts gesturing with his brief. The
    slopping out begins, a chain of prisoners moving across the
    whole stage with their buckets. All the areas start talking at
    once.*)

WARDERS: Slopping out! Slopping out!

LESTER: 'Police in the Lake District last night were refusing to
  release any further details in the case of an unemployed
  male, believed to be in his thirties, who has been arrested
  by members of the local force on a charge of interfering
  with two dolphins. It is understood that the man, whose
  identity was not disclosed, had been under surveillance
  for some time, and was finally arrested by two policemen
  who had stationed themselves with suitable breathing
  equipment at a place where they could observe the
  underwater crime. Chief Superintendent Hardy
  commended the ingenuity and perseverance of his men.
  He said that this was probably a one-off operation and he
  did not foresee that there would be any likely need for any
  further investigations of the same nature.' Well, no.
  (*Simultaneously with:*)

WOODY: Yeah, they'd delivered the brief. A bloke came

107

running round, he said, 'Have you actually got it?' I held it up, I said, 'It's in my hand . . .' He said, 'Oh God, don't tell me . . . That's forty thousand plus fifteen hundred a day.' I said, 'Yes, plus secretarial, this sort of case, don't forget, I don't have to tell you, you'll find the duplicator's running all night.' He looked at me, he said, 'Have you actually got it? In that very envelope?' He said, 'Where do you live? Have you got a garage? Do you need a new loft? What do you drive? Have you got a Jaguar?' What could I say? 'I've got a Jaguar. And I like to see Sir Peter do well.' I said, 'What can I say? You know, you delivered the brief, I hate to have to tell you, it's the custom we have. Once it's in hand, sorry, mate, more than my life's worth, once you put it in hand, you have to come through. Also, you know, there's another thing, I mean, look at it my way . . .'
(*Simultaneously with:*)

BARRY: . . . but here it's like they're saying, oh no, you know it's no good. You think, oh, if they spent half the time trying to support the actual coppers, I mean getting behind us and helping to get on with the job, if they spent half the time they do thinking up ways of not paying us, then, God knows, we'd all be much better off. Because, I tell you, there isn't a system devised, not one, not one that is conceived in the human brain that any self-respecting copper isn't going to see as a challenge and think, OK, right now, how do I get round it this time? Now look, I mean, for instance, this clothing allowance, I looked this up, look, the question of professional clothing, what you have to wear on undercover work, I mean, I can't walk into a place in my new Armani, or else my cover's blown before I even start.
(*Simultaneously with:*)

IRINA: First of these is Toby Ellington, who you will all know, who's sent a message saying, yes, this is exactly the kind of action that's needed in the legal profession, how pleased he is, and how, you know, if it were any other day, but he's of course defending in the Irish case; card here also from Lord Bethredge, who's thrilled at the idea. Also, I'm pleased to say we've had some cheques, which is excellent, from Larry Solto, of course, Jim Hail. Mary Handsworth. Basil Hart. All saying, yes, this is exactly the pressure we need to try and make sure the public understand that the legal profession at large is infinitely more sensitive and responsive than perhaps some of the more prominent dinosaurs make us appear. We do care. We are interested. We do want to see reform, and we're by no means satisfied with the lawyer's traditional image of someone who is only concerned with the administration of the law, and not with the direction it takes. Messages also from Freddy Parker . . . Bill Sopwith . . . a very nice letter here from Jane Smart . . .

(All through this, the prisoners are slopping out. As the music and crescendo of words threatens to drown everything out, SANDRA *suddenly stands up. At once the music stops, and the other areas darken. She straightens her uniform, turns and takes a few paces to the centre of the stage. She stands alone.)*

SANDRA: I want the Chief Superintendant. *(She waits.)* I wonder. Could I have a word?

(Darkness.)